NOBODY HOME

I continue
to delight in (Jan's)
humour, his clarity and his
passion for the subject of this book.
The broad scope of its content portrays the
author's deep and all encompassing
comprehension of the nature
of awakening.

TONY PARSONS,
author, *The Open Secret*

NOBODY HOME

From Belief to Clarity

JAN KERSSCHOT

New Age Books

ISBN: 81-7822-192-6

First Indian Edition: Delhi, 2005

(First published 2003 by Watkins Publishing, UK)

Published by
NEW AGE BOOKS
A-44 Naraina Phase-I
New Delhi-110 028 (INDIA)
Email: nab@vsnl.in
Website: www.newagebooksindia.com

Printed in India
at Shri Jainendra Press
A-45 Naraina Phase-I, New Delhi-110 028

Contents

ACKNOWLEDGEMENTS

I would like to express my gratitude to Lou Monte, who helped me in reviewing the manuscript, and to all who have inspired me in writing this book, especially Nathan Gill and Tony Parsons.

JAN KERSSCHOT, JANUARY 2002

Foreword

Trying to understand our way to enlightenment is as futile as trying to fit the ocean into a jam jar. It is the very effort of seeking that obstructs the seeing of that which already is. It seems that many 'spiritual teachers' still communicate the idea of a personal path of purification that can lead to a goal on a distant horizon. This is a popular message which draws big audiences. However, there is a gentle but growing interest in non-dualism, and there are those who are courageous and clear enough to communicate this simple and radical message in uncompromising terms. Jan Kersschot is one of them.

The broad scope of his book portrays the author's deep and all-encompassing comprehension of the nature of awakening. When reading a book of this kind, it is good to attempt to read between the lines – to look for what is beyond the words. Jan is aware of this and writes in such a way as to take the reader into a vision that is beyond the mind. So enjoy the adventure, and the profundity of expression, and perhaps something will resonate and another possibility will arise.

TONY PARSONS, AUTHOR OF *THE OPEN SECRET* AND *AS IT IS*

Preface

In *Nobody Home* Jan directs us to the recognition of our true nature, making clear the futility of seeking a future projected enlightenment. There may be a glimpse of the transcendental aspect of our nature as Consciousness which is then conceptualised as an ideal permanent state to be attained.

We are all the very same One. There is only Consciousness. This present appearance just as it is – including any sense of separation or ego and any search for transcendence or liberation – is already the perfect expression of life. Acceptance of this, of your nature as Consciousness, whatever presently appears in and as awareness, undermines the movement to transcend separation, ego or anything else. No particular state, condition or experience is necessary.

Fear, separation, individuality, ego, bliss, oneness, love – all is the endless play of possibility. As Jan points out, in terms of an assumed conceptual self that hopes one day to be annihilated in the attainment of 'enlightenment' is concerned, there is actually already nobody home. There is simply this present expression of, and as, what is, including any sense of presently appearing as a somebody, which is perfectly OK.

In the absence of seeking for wholeness, life is recognised as the expression of what is already whole. You, Consciousness are the object of your own game of seeking and *Nobody Home* is an exploration of this extraordinary paradox.

NATHAN GILL, AUTHOR OF *CLARITY*

INTRODUCTION

This book can be used as an initiation into a new way of seeing, into the recognition that there is another possibility, which simply transforms everything. When we neglect all belief and hearsay and find out for ourselves, we may taste this essence that does not require either the religious or the philosophical. We do not have to become special or spiritual in any way in order to reveal this open secret: everyone is invited to come Home. And 'Home' is given a capital to emphasize its infinite and impersonal quality – not to suggest it is something holy or exclusive. The Liberation I point to in this book is not just for the saints or the lucky ones: it is here for all of us. The reader will discover that nobody is excluded: the essence of its message is right here, available for you and me. And although nothing 'mystical' ever happened to me, there is a vision that I want to share with you in this book. Something utterly simple and at the same time capable of ending your spiritual quest.

When you still think of yourself as being a spiritual seeker looking for the all-encompassing truth, you are invited to have a closer look at your spiritual search. You will be asked where you think you are going. You will also be invited to check if there really is a seeker reading these very words. And making this whole issue clear, for example by taking away all your concepts about a future projected enlightenment once and for all, may be mind-blowing.

Still, I cannot guarantee that reading this book is going to bring you new philosophical insights or take away your problems. I don't promise you any mystical experiences or personal achievements on the spiritual path. If you are graced with transcendental experiences in your life, enjoy them while they seem to happen, but forget about them as soon as possible. Claiming transcendental events for yourself is a subtle trap in this matter. By reducing the Impersonal to something personal, such Grace is turned into a curse. This is also the case when you read about the mystical experiences claimed by some spiritual teachers. When you compare yourself with them, you are trapped again. Let me tell you that all those personal adventures some 'spiritual heroes' refer to are not relevant: it is all food for the thinking mind, and a very intelligent way of the ego to postpone its own unmasking. You are only fooling yourself by doing so. What we are cannot be personalized, 'It' cannot be put into a future projected state. However, if the habit of personalizing 'It' really drops away, if we stop projecting 'It' into the future, the Awareness which is witnessing all this may be recognized. Then, your spiritual seeking may come to an end. Nothing can be claimed, nothing is attained. It all happens beyond your control. Still there is Freedom because plain ordinary life is enough now. And there is absolutely no need any more to enhance day-to-day life with religious or spiritual 'stuff'. In a way, you are back where you started.

Now, what is the point of all this? There is no point to it, really, except that you are released from the stress of pursuing an ideal. You understand the meaninglessness of improving yourself, because just as you are *is* the divine expression. There is no need for religious ceremonies or spiritual exercises. Burning incense is as divine as waiting for a bus or walking in a park. You understand now it is not necessary to be continually in an ego-less state expressing divine love. You realize there is no need to achieve higher powers or to open your third eye. And it is a release to understand that nothing can be excluded: you see, moments of ordinariness are now equal to moments of bliss. The hope to 'get enlightened one day' is completely gone now since life – as it is presenting itself to you right now – is already 'It'. Sitting here and reading this is your way of expressing the Infinite. You don't have to become holy!

And so you are back into the game of ordinary life, while at the same time you see that there is nowhere to go to find 'It'. All your past efforts to attain spiritual freedom now appear as one big joke. How can somebody else teach you to be what you are? Who can show you the way back home, if you are already Home? And if you are looking for the all-encompassing, where should you go if it is *everywhere*? There is simply no escape. If the infinite is timeless, why are you still seeking? And if it is finally recognized that there is no seeker, who is going to do the seeking? Who is still there? You see, it is not *you* going Home, it is Awareness rediscovering Itself. So there is nobody going Home: Consciousness *is* already Home.

JAN KERSSCHOT,
JANUARY 2002

www.kersschot.com

If you're looking to find the key to Liberation, there is some bad news and some good news. The bad new is: there is no key to Liberation. The good news is: the door has been left unlocked.

1

WHAT ARE WE LOOKING FOR?

In the beginning there was desire,
which was the first seed of mind.
Sages, having meditated in their hearts,
have discovered by their wisdom
the subtle connection of the existent with the non-existent.

HYMN OF CREATION, THE RIG VEDA

Our true nature

The mystical is not
how the world is,
but that it is.

LUDWIG WITTGENSTEIN

All great mystics throughout human history have repeated that we may be offered insight into our True Nature if we are able to let go the concepts we have about ourselves, and just go with the evidence of our own direct experience. They insist that it can become a heartfelt challenge to awaken to a deeper essence, and that true fulfilment is only to be found after rediscovering what they call 'our true identity'. We call this a rediscovery because we will not discover something new, but we will come home to that which is always there: this present-moment awareness.[1] And maybe we will see that this present-moment awareness is the essence of our life. And at the same time we realize that this deeper essence is also the actual source of true fulfilment.

There are still a few questions. Can we believe the mystics and seers when they say that this True Essence is the source of present-moment fulfilment? And is there really such a deeper essence? What if all of this is just a new belief system? Does this so-called mystical truth that goes beyond the concepts of mind really exist? And would it be possible that 'normal' people like you and me can discover this Secret? If we want to explore this issue, we really have to start from zero. Extremely simple questions need an answer. Here are a few to start with. What makes it possible to be aware of ourselves? Who is this person we take ourselves to be? Where do our thoughts come from? And what is the core of our existence?

This is what this book is about: allowing direct recognition of our deepest centre, becoming aware of the very ground of our being. Mystics and saints say that this Essence is the source of true fulfilment, and suggest that everybody is capable of reaching this Essence. And we will check if that is really true or not. Although it may look reckless and ambitious, in this book we really want to go for this challenge: not just talking or thinking about this Essence but really seeing it! We hope to make this journey practicable through a series of awareness-experiments.[2] The practical part is for those readers who have 'forgotten' their true nature completely. No matter how clever or spiritual they think they are, they may need these artificial reminders in order to know what we are talking about. They can use these experiments to rediscover the obviousness and transparency of their 'own' awareness. For some, it may be essential to understand the rest of this book. All that the experiments require is the willingness to enquire into our own awareness until we reach the bottom line. When that line is passed, a Transparency is seen which is beyond our mental capacities. Mystics say that then our True Nature is seen.

How are we going to see our True Nature? Did our parents and teachers show us the way? Can philosophy or religion offer the key? Are contemplation, prayer or meditation the tools for going beyond the wheel of life? Will a spiritual career bring us complete salvation? Spiritual practices have been developed all over the world to assist individuals to rediscover the infinite character of our true nature. There seem to be many different ways to cross this river, and some of these paths seem to be contradictory. And there seem to be only a few able to cross that river.

There is no way to escape Presence

If the doors of perception were cleansed,
then everything would appear to man
as It is... infinite
William Blake

Seeing our True Nature is sometimes referred to as panoramic vision, in contrast to the narrow vision of the personality. Later on, we will see that this seeing is not some blissful experience nor a paranormal phenomenon, but just naked perception. It is so ordinary and so natural that we may indeed overlook it. In chapters to come, we will make clear that what we are – our True Nature – is already here anyway. So can we go and look for it? Tony Parsons writes:

> For I am already that which I seek. Whatever I seek or think I want, however long the shopping list may be, all of my desires are only a reflection of my longing to come home. And home is oneness, home is my original nature. It is right here, simply in what is. There is nowhere else I have to go, and nothing else I have to become.[3]

This quote sums up the message of this book. *Nobody Home* is indeed about rediscovering the simplicity of 'what is'. And for that, we do not need exotic meditation techniques or mystical experiences. We are not looking for a special state of mind: any state of consciousness we have will do just fine, because the very ground of our existence is fully present in every state; we can see the Transparency right now, while reading this sentence. So a change of state is not the point; recognition is the point.

Recognition of what is already the case. When we are interested in a change of state, when we are looking for a state of bliss, we are *distracted* from the all-encompassing Transparency. The joke is that we do not see 'It' because we are expecting something extraordinary *in the future*. But the truth is that It is already seen, right now. Every single bit of the true essence is fully available in our awareness right now. We just fail to recognize It. And that recognition is exactly what we will be referring to in this book.

The tendency of our mind to try and grasp this subtle state may make it look as if it is a very fleeting or extremely rare condition, but the point is that 'It' is always here. Its subtlety and ordinariness prevent us from being aware that it is always available, right here where we are. So we do not have to go anywhere to find it. Franz Kafka, the famous poet and philosopher, once said:

> You need not leave your room. Remain sitting at your table and listen. You need not even listen, simply wait. You need not even wait, just learn to become quiet, and still, and solitary. The world will freely offer itself to you to be unmasked.

SEEING OUR TRUE NATURE

> ***Throughout my early life I felt that there was another possibility which, once realized, would transform all and everything.***[4]
>
> **TONY PARSONS**

Since time immemorial, all kinds of religious and philosophical systems have dealt with fundamental questions. Is there a meaning to life? What is it to be able to say, 'I am?' Why is there suffering? How can people discover their true nature? Is it utopian to rediscover the source of inner peace and to live from that perspective a worldly life? And eventually show other people the way to this source of true contentment? Many stories about the lost paradise, about the belief in a higher power, about mystical experiences, illustrate this eternal searching. And if the mystics and seers can be believed, this 'Liberation' should be available to every human being.

We have always had an inner desire to rise above the ordinary, to overcome the limitations of the human body. Especially art illustrates this common desire to discover the mystery of our human existence. And although these expressions come in very different ways, the common ground is always the same. Paintings, sculptures and religious texts, originating from different cultures and traditions, are often the expression of this human longing for salvation. When we admire the erotic sculptures of the temples of Kajuraho in northern India, we can easily notice the peaceful expression of inner peace, joy and harmony we also recognize in Buddhist sculptures on the walls of Wat Yet Yot, the temple of the seven towers in Chiang-Mai, northern Thailand. Once we have recognized this common field, we can also see 'It' in a twentieth-century abstract painting of Mark Rothko as well as in a poem of Rumi, the famous thirteenth-century Sufi.

But is the secret of life only available in the religious or artistic? Is the all-encompassing Energy that seems to be the core of our lives only recognizable in the mystic and the extraordinary? If we are looking for what is universal, how can anything or anyone be excluded? This book is meant for those among us who feel that there must be another way, which is both easy and accessible to anyone. Those who find the concepts of philosophers too theoretical, the visions of the mystics too exclusive and the religious paths too holy, may find in this book what they have been missing. This book gives quite a pragmatic approach and is not addressed to believers, but to investigators who are ready to go to the bottom line. Some readers will also cross that line, then we reach a Space where all words and concepts fail. However, this Space, this Consciousness is not something we can 'get', and as soon as we write or talk about this 'Consciousness', we make a concept of It. We are trying to put It into a frame, as we do with a painting. But It is not a limited object that can be framed. Consciousness is not a thing that can be owned, it is not a state of mind that can be known by a seeker. In other words: it is not a separate object that can be known by a subject. That is why Lao Tse, when writing the Tao Te Ching, started with the following words: *The Tao that can be named is not the true Tao*. And then he began writing...

OPEN BUT CRITICAL

Life that has not been examined,
is not worth living,
Life that has not been lived,
is not worth examining.

PLATO

Most seekers in their quest look for experts, for authority. Certain phrases from some mystics and seers can be used as seeds for recognition: their metaphors can be interesting points of reflection. This book is full of quotes from teachers, poets and philosophers, and in some cases we accept their ideas without any criticism simply because we see how brilliant they are. Sometimes, however, we will not accept their ideas unless we have checked them for ourselves. Any blind belief in these so-called experts or teachers may not be of great value in the long run.

We cannot accept anything just on authority. Sometimes we are more interested in who said something than in what was said, like someone who sees a beautiful painting and immediately asks, 'Who painted it?' There is a story about a wonderful Buddhist text that was read out loud by a master. At the end of the story the question immediately arose, 'Who wrote that?' The master answered, 'If I told you it was the Buddha who wrote it, I know you would admire it every morning with flowers. If I told you it was written by a patriarch, you would still respect it, but not so deeply as if the Buddha himself had written it. And if I told you that one of the monks had written it, you would not know very well what to do with this information. And if I told you that the cook had written it, you would laugh about it.'

When we look for the essence of human nature, when we look for an answer to the question, 'Who am I?' it may be a good starting point not to rely too much on what others tell us or have told us, even when they are experts in their field. If we are interested in a teaching that is supposed to bring us spiritual freedom, at least the teaching itself should be free of its own cultural wrappings. Otherwise, the teaching and the teacher will not be able to point us to real freedom.[5] Still, we can be inspired by what others have understood or experienced as long as we do not copy *their* concepts, projections or belief systems. In order to come to an 'open' attitude, we need to get rid of some conditioning, and that may be one of the goals of this book. What we are invited to do is give up all our belief systems. In this book, we are not supposed to follow the thoughts and concepts of others: we are expected to see for ourselves and rely on that.[6]

Getting rid of all these layers of belief systems and conditionings will seem to be one of the most difficult aspects of our quest. Often, it seems we hold onto concepts or ideas that supply us with a certain security. But to stubbornly hold on to something is like a closed hand: nothing goes out, we do not lose anything, of course, but there is also no space to receive something new: nothing can come in.

2

FROM OPENNESS TO IDENTIFICATION

Right now you are Consciousness,

appearing as a character in your play.

Maybe you think you need confirmation.

Forget it. Relax.

You are already that.[7]

NATHAN GILL

AS A NEWBORN

I touch the sky with my finger.
Distance is nothing but a fantasy.

WILLIAM BLAKE

Before birth, we do not realize that there is a difference between ourselves and the environment. There is no line between 'me' and 'not me'. That difference can only be noticed by an outsider, for example by a gynaecologist during an ultrasound investigation. As a newborn we are still pure awareness, a sort of clear *attention*. We do not label what is appearing in that open attention: we just let everything appear and disappear. Now the breast of our mother appears, then our little foot comes in our awareness, then the sound of a rattle, the voice and the face of the father, a feeling of hunger in the stomach. These are all sensations that come to the surface: just like in a movie, these images appear and disappear. We do not realize yet that we are a person, we do not know we have a name, a family or a nationality. We do not even know we have a body, or that we exist at all! In this so-called 'open attention' there are only 'sensations' that pass by like clouds. As a baby we do not have much self-awareness; we have not yet developed a conscious individuality. The question, 'Who am I?' is not relevant. Instead, there is only an open attention in which experiences appear and immediately disappear. There is no separation yet between the 'me' and the 'outside world'. Small children do not, for example, realize there is such a thing as 'distance': when they look through the window, an aeroplane in the air is just as large as a fly on the window glass.

Because the observations are not coloured yet by all kinds of thought patterns, a newborn still exists in unity and does not yet experience any difference between 'here' and 'there' or between 'you' and 'me'. Babies do not know yet about space or time: babies seem to live in the here and now, without the mind distracting them with concepts of what is happening. Concepts such as 'yesterday' and 'tomorrow' are also not concrete yet; the child's thinking does not yet perceive time. In other words: it is *being without knowing* and everything is still witnessed as one unity.

Moments of Dualism

An integral being
knows without going,
sees without looking,
and accomplishes without doing.

LAO TSE

As a newborn, we do not realize what it is to be a human in this world. We do not know what it is to be a person, and we do not realize that there is a planet called 'the world'. We still feel united with the environment that offers itself because there is no clearly delineated self-consciousness, but this state of unity does not last. In order to manifest ourselves in the outside world, we begin to develop a personality. This process goes hand in hand with the development of the mind, using its capacity for differentiation and its memory. These are our first steps into dualism. As soon as our thinking becomes active, the environment is cut into pieces. This is necessary to build up our rational knowledge.

When the nervous system differentiates itself further, there is a growing ability to recognize certain phenomena. 'Recognize' here means to compare with a previous image. This indicates that the memory begins to become active. We recognize the face of our mother, the colour of the feeding bottle, the softness of the teddy bear, and the thinking capacity begins to give our life its shape and content.

The birth of dualism is the beginning of mental distinctions and as such, the beginning of the battle between 'me' and the rest of the world. This is the game of separation; we start to pretend that we are limited, and we divide the world in a 'me' and a 'not-me'. The ego distinguishes and it says to itself, 'This is mine, and that is not mine'. Later on, usually around the age of two, all kinds of things and situations are further identified with the ego: my mother, my bed, my pyjamas, my doll, my foot, my arm. Automatically another world is created, an entire world of the 'not mine': not my mother, not my toy, and so forth. Around this world, step by step, an 'owner' is created with his or her own territory.

Progressively a little person is created into our mind; this ego seems to live in our head and says, 'I am a little boy or girl' and 'This body is mine'. Our mind creates a philosopher in our head, a 'thinker of thoughts'. When a thought comes to our mind, the mind claims, 'I had a thought'. When there is a bodily feeling such as pain, this thinker says, 'I have felt it'. And so we identify more and more with this person in our body who says to himself, 'I have felt it, I have thought it'. Instead of saying, 'There was pain', we start to say, 'I have pain'. Finally we identify completely with this person in our body who says to himself, 'I have attained it, I have done it'. The latter is sometimes referred to as *the sense of personal 'doership'*.[8]

The sense of personal doership is a habit that develops slowly. In most cases, it starts to arise at around the age of two or three, and reaches complete development when we are a young teenager. Slowly but progressively, we start to identify with our personality, with our image, with what we do. And, as Douglas Harding[9] puts it, we finally join the human club. When there is a strong and permanent sense of personal doership, we identify with the one who is turning around in circles, subject to the laws of cause, space and time. A whole new world – a conceptual world – is created: the child has turned into a grown-up now. In other words: the 'Being' part is still there in the background, but the 'human part' is overshadowing the original state of openness more and more.

EYE TO EYE WITH THE MIRROR

> ***When you finally find out everything you are not,***
> ***What you are left with is 'aware space'.*** [10]
>
> **ADYASHANTI**

Let us now turn back to the period where we were not yet identified with our personality. When we were very young, we regularly felt as if we were living in a magical world. We all remember those moments when we did not listen to the ego with its fears and desires, its plans and its goals. We still lived in a simple unity. For example, we did not recognize ourselves in the bathroom mirror. When others deliberately confronted us with our image, we reacted just like a cat – totally indifferent. When we became older and we saw our image reflected in the mirror, we said, 'That is my little friend'. But we did not yet claim, 'The one over there in the mirror, that is me'.

It is only after long and repetitive insistence by parents and older brothers or sisters who all say, 'That person you see in the mirror, that is you,' that we start to believe what the others have told us. Pointing at us, they say, 'You are that little boy or girl'.

Slowly, we exchange our personal view of the world as First Person, the vision in which we are open attention, to third-person vision, the vision that *others* have of us. We call it 'third-person vision' because it is a concept built up by a third party, by an outsider. In other words, the image that others have of us is becoming more and more important in building up our sense of self. At the same time, however, our 'naked awareness' is gradually overshadowed by the identification process. Instead of living from our own centre of perception, we start to imagine, under pressure from the outside world, that we live from the point of view of an imagined (third) person. In other words, we pretend to be an actor playing in front of a camera.

When our parents continue to say that we are that image in the glass there [behind that mirror], each one of us eventually believes it. Even though that image is a few metres away from us, in that other bathroom, even though the mirror image moves its right hand when we move our left hand, we have to accept this concept. At that age, we are not aware of this conditioning, although we find that for ourselves, seen from our own centre, as a First Person, we are completely different from that image in the mirror, much in the same way as our voice sounds completely different from our voice recorded by a video camera. In other words, someone else gives us a new identity by pointing at us and giving us a name.

Since the others continue to point at family pictures and movies to show us *how we look to them*, we are supposed to accept their vision and to drop our own vision of openness and clear seeing. And not only have the others given us this identification, we ourselves have also contributed to the identification process. Our own memory tells us that it is that same face that appears again and again every morning in the bathroom mirror. In fact we have taken on that mask in the mirror for ourselves.

We identify ourselves with that particular face, with that image on our passport photograph, with the attached body, with our name and even with our clothes. We forget entirely how we experience ourselves as First Person, and we exchange our first-hand living experience for what others tell us.

FURTHER IDENTIFICATION WITH OUR PERSONALITY

> *Am I a black dot on a white space*
> *or am I a white space with a black dot?* [11]
>
> CHUCK HILLIG

Just like most people, we have learned to identify with our body, with our name, with a certain type of character. Sensations such as taste, smell and touch seem to be localised in our body and these sensations seem to confirm the feeling of being locked into that bag physicians call skin. We realize more and more that we are locked into a body-mind machine.

Pleasant sensations, such as being hugged or eating chocolate, and unpleasant sensations, such as pain when being given an injection by a doctor, are registered more and more as very different sensations, which are then differentiated as such and catalogued in the central computer, the brain. Our mental computer conditions itself to say 'yes' to pleasure and enjoyment and 'no' to pain and sadness, and there is not much we can do to change that: it is just the way our genetic code and our conditioning are programmed. It is how the mind and senses work.

With the establishment of such yes-no reactions to all kinds of experiences, we create our personality, we develop its characteristics, our likes and dislikes. As a result, the role we play as an adult in society becomes more and more obvious. We delineate this role with the concept of the 'ego', although the term ego may have other meanings. In this book the ego stands for the role we play in everyday life, for the sense of personal doership, for the personality that we have identified ourselves with. One of the tools of the ego is our memory, and also the beliefs we have acquired, like the concept of right and wrong, and the belief in time and causality.

How does this so-called ego feel about itself and the world? The ego feels locked up in the body, and sees itself separate from the rest. As this separation between our 'me' and the outside world becomes increasingly clearer, we feel we have to defend ourselves. As a result, we gradually try to manifest ourselves in the outside world. Over the years, we develop new talents, we acquire our own ambitions. With this process, the ego-awareness begins to overshadow the original open awareness. The thirst to discover new things and new experiences starts to grow, the ego is more and more guided by the little voice inside. As a result, the concept of being a thinker is establishing itself more and more.

3

MOMENTS THAT GO BEYOND

Everything leads to awakening.
Even that which your mind may see as harmful
is reminding you of another possibility.
Simply give up your attachment and fascination
with the story of your personal life
and let life happen.
Something else of immense significance
will take the place of all your worries
and you will be overrun by a new sense of
wonder.
Everything will reflect a quality of benevolence.
This is the natural way for life to be.[12]

TONY PARSONS

HOW DO WE DEAL WITH MISSING OUR ORIGINAL STATE?

A sudden perception
that Subject and object are one
will lead you to a deeply mysterious
wordless understanding.
You will awaken to the truth of Zen.

HUANG-PO

As little children, we have a natural ability to access our inner Source whenever our heart whispers its necessity. Yet, as we grow older and join the human club, that whisper is often muted by a mind plagued with expectations, fears and desires. When we mature, we develop our personality and we identify ourselves more and more with it. As a result, we seem to become completely 'stuck' in our body-mind machine. And this personality really wants to become a full member of the club of adults. Of course our identification with the body and mind is essential for developing into a normal adult with a healthy personality; it is an essential step in the evolution from baby to grown-up. Without our rational mind, a normal life in this world as an adult is not possible. But at the same time, this identification process has caused us to lose our access to the original state of open awareness. Would it be possible to rediscover our original state and live from that vision, without having to sacrifice the qualities of our personality? In other words, can we have the best of both worlds? Can we rediscover the openness from our early childhood without becoming childish? Can we transcend the thinking mind without becoming insane? Can we rediscover the core of true spirituality without becoming a priest? These may be crucial questions for those among us who do not wish to give up worldly life for a spiritual life, for those who want to live a 'normal' life in western society and still hope to have a vision that includes the infinite in that same everyday life.

To further explain this, we have to make a (theoretical) distinction between two visions. We will call them vision X and vision Y. The first vision is the 'human' vision we achieve while growing up. It is the perspective of common sense. We call this concept 'vision X'. It is the vision everybody believes in. Vision X is the perspective of the grown-ups, based on the belief that we are separate entities living and moving on the planet. But there is another perspective; it concerns the awareness we were talking about before. We call this second perspective 'vision Y'. The latter is the 'vision' of the newborn. It is also referred to as our 'original nature'. According to vision Y, what we really are is open attention, and all the concepts about ourselves and the world are mere illusions *appearing in that same awareness*. It is sometimes referred to as 'naked awareness' or 'childlike innocence' since we were not spoiled yet by the concepts and belief systems of society.

What are the differences between these two visions? There are two main differences. First, vision X is dualistic in nature, while vision Y is non-dualistic. And second, vision X is a practical tool to live as a human being in society, while vision Y is completely useless. Vision Y has no value but for explaining the perspective we want to present in this book. In other words, vision Y is only significant when we are looking for our true nature.

VISION X	VISION Y
dualistic	non-dualistic
grown-up	newborn
identification	open Attention
limited	infinite

Vision X and vision Y seem to be diametrically opposite to one another, but later in this book we will see that vision X is in fact only a part of vision Y. In other words, vision X is the personal or limited version and vision Y is the all-encompassing One, as is illustrated in the drawing below. And since 'It' is without boundaries, it is impersonal and infinite, and referred to as Oneness. 'It' is borderless. To make clear It is infinite, we always write It with a capital. Other descriptions we will use in this book are: Home, Source, Original Face, the Light, and so on.

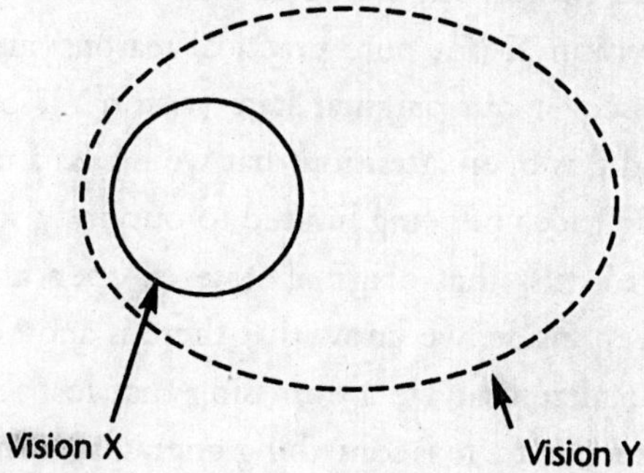

SANDCASTLES ON THE BEACH

There is no way to Happiness.
Happiness is the way.

GAUTAMA BUDDHA

To illustrate the concept of vision X and vision Y, we can use the metaphor of building sandcastles on the sandy beach. Vision X corresponds with our sense of being limited to our body and mind. In other words, we feel like a sandcastle. Vision Y is the open attention of the newborn baby: it is the naked awareness we are born with. It corresponds with the limitless nature of the sand on the sandy beach.

Although the sandcastle is made of the same sand as the other sandcastles, each castle feels separate from the others. But if one particular castle thinks it is a spiritual seeker, it definitely wants to get a taste again of its limitless nature. The question is now if we (as a castle) can rediscover our essence, being grains of sand. In other words: can we be both sandcastle and sand? Can we keep vision X (for pure practical reasons) and at the same time rediscover our original state (vision Y)? Since we have exchanged this open attention that we had as a newborn baby for the adult idea of being limited to our body, sooner or later we start to miss that original state of open attention. Somewhere deep inside, we know that there is another possibility and we realize that we are missing that lost feeling of Oneness. We feel that there is something ungraspable far beyond what we know. Deep inside there is a longing for that mystery of Openness we had as a newborn. And this longing for fulfilment directs our search for ultimate transcendence. If we did not have this longing for the ultimate, we would not be sitting here reading this book. Nobody needs to tell us that there is more to life than what we see and feel in everyday living. In other words, we are a spiritual seeker. We know that there is 'more' and that finding It will give us inner fulfilment.

When we feel that there is something fundamental missing, when we realize this, we may feel melancholic or frustrated. Or we may start looking for our original state of bliss and peace, although we do not know what we are looking for. There are many possibilities here. Some among us may look for a more spiritual life because they feel that the material world is no longer satisfying; they yearn for a higher dimension, they long for a life that goes beyond the ordinary daily life. Others try to give new meaning to their life by looking for a social task, or by looking for a religious career. Or we may do the opposite by trying to compensate the loss of spiritual richness by looking for happiness in the outside world. And some among us may feel the need for material, emotional or mental satisfaction in some way or another. Without realizing that the true reason for this need is the fact that we have lost conscious contact with our Source, we crave power, money, attention, love, recognition. And we are willing to manipulate ourselves and the others in order to get what we need. Instead of living a natural life from within, we live a life according to the standards of society, according to the expectations created by education or advertising, and we start to compare our situation with the social or material situation of the people around us. As a result, we may look for control over others, we seek power. In other words, we want our castle to be bigger than the other castles. We develop a personality that gets respect for its intelligence, or for its position in society. In order to further build up this feeling of power, we may additionally look for an identification with something larger than ourselves, such as a professional society, a football team, a political party, a nation or a religion. Nothing is wrong with all these mechanisms, but we should realize that some of them are a compensation for a deeper need.

One day we realize that indeed both material and social success are temporary and that sooner or later we will have to give up what we have built up. We will have to give up some parts of it as we grow older and the rest of it when we die. If all these processes serve to replace a sense of lack within our inner self, we may better understand why we live such an egocentric life. This egocentric life – materialistic or spiritual – may indeed be an attempt to regain our Original State: we are, without realizing it, desperately in search of that original feeling of transparency, oneness and simplicity. And when we realize that this so-called egocentric game may have its origins in losing contact with our Essence, we also understand it would be far more interesting to go for the inner Source directly.

BEFORE THE MIND

If you do not look within,
if you do not look without,
what remains? Be that.[13]

MIRA PAGAL

There are moments in our life when we realize that some concepts we took for real are not so certain and obvious at all. There were many such moments especially in our childhood when we were totally absorbed in what was happening. These borderline moments are, for instance, those times when we are carefree, sitting in the sun, just like that. We are without thought, completely absorbed by our environment: the grass, the trees, the wind, our arms, our legs, it is all connected, it is all one field of awareness. These are experiences we have at the edge of our thinking and feeling capacities.

Even as grown-ups, we may have similar moments of being absorbed, moments of blind faith in what is going on: for example when we stare into an open fire, when we are hypnotised on the beach by the sounds and colours of the surf. When we devote ourselves completely to a game, when we admire a sunset, or when we play a musical instrument, we can truly lose ourselves. Afterwards, when we reflect on the moment, we say, 'Oh, I wasn't with it', or 'I just wasn't there'. Without realizing it at that moment, we were absorbed in an endless space where everything seemed to happen without effort. Our thinking process slowed down and we limited ourselves to a bland observing, a watching without judging. There was just peace of mind. No matter if we were active or not, there was a stillness in the background that permeated everything. And there was also no complaining, no urge to change people or things. Often, those moments were very peaceful and fulfilling.

What is important here is that we can notice that each time we are really happy, truly fulfilled, there is no thinking process going on. There is just 'what is'. The thinking mind only pops up *afterwards*. When there is no thinking process going on, there is no hope and no fear, no complaining, no desire and no guilt. Later in this book, we will see that during such moments, there is no identification with our personality. In other words, there is no 'me'. And we can check for ourselves if it is true that each time there is real happiness, that there is in fact *nobody there*. No separation, no self-image, just pure being. There is only pure 'Is-ness' which is not disturbed by any concept or thought about our little me. There is just *aware Space*.

This is a preview of what it must be like to be in contact

with our Essence, to come Home to our Self. All the daily worries that keep us going are melting away. When ignoring the turbulence of our internal dialogue, when going beyond the habit of identifying with our personality, we may get connected with the infinite. This is often combined with a purity and openness we have not known since our early youth.

WHO IS IT THAT EXPERIENCES OUR LIFE?

That which is essential
is invisible to the eye.

ANTOINE DE SAINT-EXUPÉRY

With such moments of purity and openness in mind, some fundamental questions may come to the surface and be looked at from a new perspective. What is our true essence? Where does a thought go after it disappears? Within what is everything appearing? Who experiences our sensations? Who is looking through our eyes? When we look at images passing, is there any evidence of eyes that are looking? Can we say that the optical nerves are doing the watching? When we take a look at our hand right now, is there any evidence of brain cells that are looking? Scientists say that the light of the sun reflects on the skin of our hand to stimulate light-sensitive cells at the back of our eyeballs; an electric current then leads this information to a specific part of the brain, which gives – and this is the magic and unexplained step – a specific image of our hand in our awareness.

So where is the observation happening exactly? It is hard to spot the exact location of the visual process. And we can ask ourselves if there is any evidence of a person who is observing.

Maybe it is just a blank screen filled with mental images. Although we can not touch this white canvas, this empty screen is aware of the images that appear and disappear on it. We will go into this subject again in chapters to come.

When we listen to sounds, can we say who is listening? Is there any evidence of ears that are hearing? On present evidence, is it a specific area in the brain that is performing the listening? Is there any evidence of a person who is hearing? Or is it just silence filled with sounds, with vibrations? Although we cannot experience it, this silence is aware of the sounds that come and go. Would it be possible to hear this silence?

When we take this book in our hands, do we actually feel the paper or do we feel what is going on in our fingertips? Let us do a little experiment and try to look for ourselves. We close our eyes and we move our fingertips over the paper of this book right now, and observe what happens. Who is experiencing these sensations? When we say we feel a piece of paper between our thumb and forefinger, who (or what) is feeling that? Is it our nervous system? And where exactly are these sensations happening? In our fingertips? In our brain cells? In our mind? We may say, 'I am feeling it', but is that really true? And who or what is this 'I am'?

We live in a world of perceptions, be it coming from the so-called outside world or coming from the so-called inside world, our body. That is why we could say that this world we seem to live in is an illusion, a daydream. We are all free to believe in the reality of our daydream, but in fact we can never give direct proof of the reality of which we perceive. And we are invited to check that out right now. Where is the so-called outside world when we are in deep sleep? Where would the world be if our senses are not functioning? Some philosophers and mystics say that indeed there is no world apart from our mind. They say, 'Nothing is left when the mind is not functioning'. That is why they suggest that this so-called outside world is nothing but a product of our senses of our mind. And why it is sometimes referred to as an illusion, created by our own ideas and thoughts.[14]

When we suggest that this world we think we live in is an illusion, we do not mean that this world does not exist, but that this world does not exist as an entity that is separate from awareness. The visual world is on our retinas, projected in space and time on a mental screen. And the same goes for the other senses. In other words: what we perceive is in fact a mental construction of our own mind. We perceive the so-called outside world through a stream of mental images that appear in our awareness. We can of course not deny the objects that we perceive, we can not deny the physical sensations in our body, but all these perceptions can not be proved to exist when not perceived.

When we are reading the words in this book right now, who is it that understands the meaning of these words? When we answer that it is our mind that analyses the meaning of these words, what is it that is aware of the concept 'our mind'? As soon as we try to get to the bottom of these questions, we end up with a paradox: who is aware of the mind? It is difficult for our mind to answer that question, because that which observes can not be analysed. It is our mind itself that makes us believe there is a mind. But our personality will not give up and will for instance say, 'I am my mind; I am perceiving it', without explaining who or what is this 'I am'.

Still, we can not deny that we are aware. This awareness is not something that can be understood by our mind because it is beyond conceptual understanding. It is not a concept, a feeling, not even a state of mind. Rather than being yet another image appearing on the TV screen, it is the screen itself. Seers and mystics say that this awareness or consciousness is the light that makes our lives shine, the ground of our being, our true Essence.

UNVEILING CONSCIOUSNESS

> ***You can't move away from It***
> ***because the very movement away from It***
> ***is It.***[15]
>
> **TONY PARSONS**

What is the missing gap between what we really are and what we think or believe we are? What is the missing link that transcends this dualism? Where is the background that unifies everything? Why did we lose this basic sense of Openness? One of the reasons is that most people seem not to notice Awareness itself. The way we experience the 'material' world is like a surface phenomenon, like ripples on the surface of a lake. These ripples come and go, but the vastness of Being is not bothered with the shape and characteristics of the ripples. We do not notice that which notices because our mind has the tendency to be distracted by the objective contents of consciousness like bodily sensations, feelings and thoughts. All these incoming data overshadow the noticing of the context of consciousness, namely Awareness itself. In other words: we see the images on the screen, but do not notice the white screen itself. We are hypnotized by the story of the actors, and forget the omnipresent energy of the Light that makes our movies visible. Some spiritual teachers say that this background of awareness is what we really are. Why do most spiritual seekers find it difficult to accept that? Is there a reason why we do not see this? Is it because we lack the direct experience of naked awareness? How can we find a solution for this?

Let us start with a basic element: the sense of being a conscious human being. Indeed, one of the certainties we all have is the fact that we exist. Everybody can say, 'I am'. Without any doubt, we can state, 'I am present, I am here', or 'Right now, while reading these very words, I am aware that I am'.

The question is: where does this 'I-am-certainty' come from? Well, it comes from Awareness Itself. It is Awareness becoming conscious of Itself through this recognition. So, it is not 'me' discovering Awareness, it is not a personal process; it is Awareness discovering Itself. Most people can get a taste of this non-duality during a so-called peak-experience, and some also sense the perfume of its impersonal nature, but this is just the beginning. If we investigate the source of this background, we will find a 'naked awareness' that is not based on a sensation or a thought. This 'I am' is not based on the knowledge of the mind or upon any of the senses, although one could say that at the same time It is the very essence of all our knowledge. When we see this clearly, we put in perspective the words of the French philosopher René Descartes (1596–1650), who said: 'I think, therefore I am'. Such a statement originates from the common belief that thinking equals Being. This is a very common idea in Western philosophy. We should remember that *before* we can think, we must be aware. First there is 'naked Being,' then all the rest follows. Even identification with the thinking mind comes after Being. First there is a white paper, than there are the words, and not the other way round. First an empty screen, then the thoughts about myself appearing on that screen. So, a different way of putting his statement would be 'I am, therefore I think'.

What can we say about this background of Awareness? When we take a look at the western philosophical and psychological approaches to the nature of mind and its relation to the body, we will have to conclude that most authors do not mention 'naked awareness' at all. They usually do not recognize awareness as existing in its own right. On the contrary, the phenomenon of naked awareness is usually confused with a specific state of mind (e.g. during deep sleep or meditation) that goes with a certain type of electric activity of the brain (as is demonstrated by electroencephalographic research). An explanation may be that these authors are excellent in analysing brain waves (or brain scans) but do not have any 'experience' with naked awareness themselves. Still, some authors – especially those coming from the East – report the existence of 'naked awareness'. Most of them are not neuroscientists and have no medical or scientific background. Some of them claim that they have 'seen' consciousness without its content. Several seers and mystics, coming from completely different traditions (Taoism, Advaita Vedanta, Zen Buddhism, Sufism), also speak of experiencing consciousness without objects. Could it be possible that this 'naked awareness' is also available to you and me?

IN CONTACT WITH THE MYSTERIOUS ESSENCE

We shape clay into a pot,
but it is the emptiness inside
that holds whatever we want.

TAO TE CHING

Every person has a certain experience of the ineffable, of the mysterious ground with which we are in contact. Although we all pretend to be separate individuals, there is a deeper intelligence that knows that we are 'connected' to each other and to the rest of the Universe. When we look at the stars at night, we simply feel that we are so much more than a body-mind machine. Many people have seen this universal wisdom, and have confirmed that we are so much wider than what we *think* we are. To some people, this secret seems to reveal itself in so-called mystical experiences, and those people who are capable of putting this mystery into words are known as mystics or seers. The descriptions of their experiences are fascinating sources of inspiration for the seeker on the spiritual path. Many who have gone before us have also searched for the essence of humankind. They have looked for the source of our consciousness, and they have tried to share their vision. Several of these mystical experiences brought a universal wisdom to the surface, a knowing which was independent of who had the mystical experience. The common field in all these stories is quite fascinating. All these stories can be supplementary guidelines for the answers to our own questions.

What is a so-called mystical experience? The mystical experience is sometimes described as the apprehension of an ultimate unity in all things, a oneness to which neither the senses nor the reason can penetrate. There is no awareness of self, only consciousness of Unity. Subject and object merge and there is only oneness. The fact that nothing is seen or heard distinguishes it from visionary experiences or telepathic communication. Thus mysticism [in this narrower sense] is not concerned with the acquisition and development of unusual powers, control of hidden forces or access to special revelations. Although mystical experiences are often unsolicited and occur spontaneously, many disciplines have been devised to prepare the aspirant for mystical union.[16] Many of these disciplines, both Eastern and Western, were absorbed in organised religions, and presented as tools for spiritual liberation. All these stories can be interesting points of interest, but they easily become side tracks when we are looking for our true nature.

In this book, we do not want to copy the mystical path of one specific tradition. We aim for a vision that is not dependent on any tradition, therefore we must look for that level where we rise above symbolic dogmatism. In other words, we must look for that place where different traditions intersect. When these mystic images are disentangled as much as possible from their religious interpretation, we will reach a platform where the different paths meet. We are aiming for the common truth that is not dependent on one specific spiritual tradition. Whichever path we have used to climb to reach the top becomes irrelevant. This platform is not the end of our quest, but it may become a perfect starting point to that 'other' dimension, to a level that is beyond dualities. In order to discourage people from imagining a sort of paradise on top of that imaginary hill, we can also use the metaphor of peeling the onion, as the latter does not promise a goal to be attained but suggests how we have to let go concept after concept. Just like peeling an onion layer by layer, we may discover that at the end we find nothing at all.

DWELLING IN THE WITNESS

He who knows the always-so,
has room in him for everything.

LAO TSE

When we look at the thoughts arising in our mind, they are like images passing by on a screen. We may notice various ideas, symbols, concepts, desires and fears, all spontaneously arising in our awareness. When we welcome bodily sensations, feelings and thoughts without judging them, without trying to control them, we put less focus on what appears on the screen and we may get a 'sense' of the Light in which they appear. When we witness all these sensations passing by, without fighting the pain and without trying to prolong the pleasure, they are simply faced on the spot, as they appear. When taking notice of them like that, we just see them, recognize them and let them move on. As when watching a movie, the images come up, stay for a moment, and then disappear.

The point we want to make here is that if we can witness all these perceptions passing by, can we then also say that we *are* these perceptions? Can we notice something and be it at the same time? Can an object also be the subject of that object? Can a cloud see itself passing by in the blue sky? No, of course not. So we can see the clouds float by because we are not those clouds: what we are is the witnessing of those clouds. What we are is the Subject that notices all these objects. In other words, we are the Light in the images. Spontaneously and naturally, these perceptions all arise in this ever-present awareness, and disappear again.

All the things we know about ourselves are objects in our awareness. How old we are, what we look like, our nationality, our name, our personal characteristics, they are images parading by in front of our awareness. The same goes for our feelings. So, in the end, who are we? If we are not those objects out there, if we are not those passing thoughts, who or what are we in essence? In fact, we can say: 'I have feelings, but I am not those feelings. I have desires, but I am not those desires. I think that I have a personality, but I am not that particular personality. What I am is the witnessing of this body, the witnessing of this personality.'

When we dwell in this witnessing, we discover a field that has a familiar quality. This witnessing may sound cold and impersonal, but it is closer to our true nature than anything else. Seeing this witnessing – if we can put it that way – has a very familiar perfume. When this 'field' is seen, we have to admit that 'It' is more 'me' than our usual (conceptual) sense of self. That is why we say that we come Home to ourselves. Many seekers say that this recognition can also give a strong sense of freedom or inner release, but this witnessing awareness is not itself anything specific we can see. It is just a vast emptiness in which our manifest world arises. All great seers throughout history have said this, and it is up to us to verify it. If we can have a look at our ego, we have to conclude that we cannot *be* the ego. The personality is seen in awareness, along with all other perceptions. So, the personality cannot be that awareness, cannot be our True Self. In other words: what we *know* cannot be what we are, and what we *are* can never be known. This idea is so obvious, and still there is a lot of confusion about this, especially in western philosophy. It is important that we notice the difference between subject and object – what we *really are* and what we *perceive* about our body and personality. Many objects and concepts can arise in the Subject, we can perceive a wide range of bodily sensations, we can notice many different aspects of our personality, and we can bring all these perceptions together in one concept called 'my ego', but we can never say that our ego is the final Subject: our ego is just another object perceived. The image we have in our mind about ourselves is just a mental object, appearing and disappearing. As a result, it is not the final Perceiver. Although we consider the body and mind and all our characteristics as very personal, they are but images passing by. And these images are not our true Identity, are they?

4

SEEING OR BELIEVING

As I walked my spiritual path
I passed many signposts
left by seekers who had
passed this way before me.
All pointed onward to the Truth.
Camped at the base of each
was a mass of people
who had stopped
and were now worshipping
the sign.[17]

WAYNE LIQUORMAN

LET US BE PRACTICAL

Cease overlooking this terribly neglected spot,
this centre-point of our life,
which on inspection instantly explodes into the universe,
and all will come clear.

DOUGLAS HARDING

As mentioned before, both a theoretical and a practical approach are offered in this book, therefore a number of experiments will be presented. On the one hand, we are invited to do these experiments with an open attitude, with a childlike innocence. The meaning of the experiments cannot be understood by the grasping mind of the adult. What we are pointing at in this chapter is a sense of perception we already 'had' as a newborn. The difference is that at that age, we were not aware of it. On the other hand, we are not going to believe anything on authority, so we will aim in our search to combine two ways of seeing, namely to look at the world with the openness of a newborn and with the critical sense of a scientist. In wonder and at the same time soberly observing, we can see that the simplest things in our daily existence are very special. This demands of the reader both an eagerness to discover and a wakefulness to observe by direct experience. This requires a certain form of simplicity as well as sensibility. Without this attitude, the experiments will have no effect. Even though the experiments look very simple, complete openness is necessary. Nobody else can help us to make the final step. Reading about it will not be enough. Even if someone puts a cup of tea in front of our mouth, it is still up to us to swallow it and get the taste of it.

Most of the experiments in this book are based on the workshops of Douglas Harding and are designed to get a taste of 'our' naked Awareness.[18] They invite us to awaken, within the present moment, into a natural recognition of our true nature. This awakening may lead to an understanding of the fundamental and essential nature of our human Beingness and cast new light on how we experience ourselves as a human being. But this will not happen if we cannot set aside our normal consensus-based assumptions about ourselves. For at least a moment, we have to forget our concepts about ourselves and the world we live in. In other words, we should be able to put in perspective our ideas about the so-called apparent objectivity of the external reality (the world we think we live in) and of the internal self (the perceptions we have of our body).

Letting go all our concepts, even just for a second, is not easy. That is one of the reasons why most people do not 'see' the naked awareness the first time they try one of the experiments. As long as they are not able to take off their sunglasses, they will not get a glimpse of this clear vision. These readers will wonder what these silly experiments are all about, and as a result, they will not get the point of this book. But they should not give up immediately. The transparency we talk about will come to the surface most unexpectedly, be it during one of the coming experiments or just like that, spontaneously. Many people who try the experiments complain that nothing seems to happen. When people say that they do not see It, they generally mean that they do not feel It: this inner Source of clear awareness leaves them indifferent because It is not a sensational happening. We could even say that this Centre of awareness is completely featureless.

Seeing this Centre is not a matter of feeling but of simply being. One could say that a veil of fog disappears. All that happens is an unveiling of our naked Consciousness and some people report that this goes with a sense of weightlessness, a sense of absence, but also of fullness. Seeing our naked awareness is certainly not in itself a mystical or religious experience, not a sudden euphoric expansion into universal love or cosmic consciousness. Quite the contrary, it is absolutely neutral. Usually, mystical experiences are considered as moments of grace, flashes of revelation that are not only rare, but only available to a small minority of the population. In mystic and spiritual literature, they seem to be exclusively accessible to saints and seers. It is therefore remarkable that we are going to do a number of experiments to immediately enable us, here and now, to come in direct contact with this other dimension. And everybody is invited to take a look.

SIMPLE AWARENESS

The foolish deny what they see,
not what they think.
The wise reject what they think,
not what they see.

HUANG-PO

What is it like to be aware of our naked consciousness? Suddenly, we realize that it is a wonder to be able to say, 'I am aware'. We are conscious that we are aware. As we said before, all of us can say, 'I am', without any hesitation. Even though this discovery seems minimal at first, it is a revolution with unimaginable consequences. As an experiment, we can start by just being aware of the world around us. When we look out at the immediate environment, we can let our mind and the environment mix. We forget about ourselves and just allow what is happening. We can notice objects around us, see their colour or structure and we can see that it takes no effort on our part to let this witnessing happen. Instead of looking at things, we let things look at us. This passive mode of looking around may bring to the surface a new kind of being: we realize our present awareness, in which these images are floating. It all comes quite naturally. It is like noticing the white paper we are writing our perceptions on. And later on we may also notice that this awareness is always available, even when we are not noticing this witnessing. We simply witness that there is an effortless awareness of what is on show right now.

When we draw attention to the sensations in our body, we can be aware of whatever bodily feelings are present; for example the pressure on our buttocks where we are sitting on a chair, maybe pain in our neck or low back. Whether these feelings are comfortable or not, we can easily be aware of them. Even when we feel too tired or too lazy to check this, we can effortlessly notice this tiredness or laziness. All these sensations arise in our present awareness. This field of consciousness is crystal clear and is witnessing the sensations in our body in an effortless and spontaneous way. Now, the next issue is: are we the witnessing awareness or are we the person we always believe we are? Which one is the 'closest' to ourselves: the author on the screen or the screen itself? Which one is more *me*, the personality that is playing a role or the Light that makes this person visible? Isn't it true that we have to 'be' before we can believe we are a personality? Which one comes first? Which one deserves the title 'me'?

When we see that in the first place we are the Light, we also know that we are making room for our personality to come to the surface. We are 'availability' for our thoughts and feelings.

Our mind and body appear in that same 'availability', and this awareness is the core of our Being. That is why mystics and seers say that this naked awareness is what we really are. Realizing this, can we still state that we are in a body, or should we say that our body is appearing in us? When looking carefully, we can notice that our body appears to us as a series of sensory perceptions and as a series of concepts we have about ourselves. We know our body because we feel parts of it: we know we have a back when we have low back pain, we realize that we have teeth when we have toothache, and so on. And we also have (indirect) knowledge about ourselves through concepts: we know what we look like because we remember our image in the mirror or because we remember our appearance from photographs. The same idea goes for our character: people have told us that we are egocentric, melancholic, optimistic, or whatever. Or we may imagine that we are intelligent or impatient. Although all these labels may just have temporary validity, we accept them as the *permanent* characteristics of our body and mind. Putting all this together (using our memory) we get an image of ourselves we call our personality.

As adults, we have learned to *identify* with these sensations and qualities, with all these concepts about ourselves. Although the idea of being a personality is in itself no more than another image passing by, we have convinced ourselves that this personality with all its characteristics is what we really are. But when we look very carefully, we may see that these sensations do not appear in our body, nor in our brain, but in our conscious attention. We are told by scientists that consciousness is a function emerging from the brain, an organ of our body. But when we dare to look ourselves, we may see that it is just the opposite: we do not appear in our mind or in our body, they *appear in us*. Or in other words, our body and mind appear as images in our aware attention, like clouds passing by in the sky, or ripples on a lake.

SHIFT OF ATTENTION

God has focused the senses to the outside,
therefore man looks outside, not inside.
Now and then an adventurous soul,
in search of immortality,
has looked back and found himself.

KATHA UPANISHAD

When we want to transcend our senses, we face a major problem: we cannot explain it in a book. What we are pointing at here is something that we cannot learn as we learned algebra or how to drive a car. It cannot be made up by the mind; instead, it is a very subtle transformation, something that can only be welcomed. It is not accessible using concentration, we cannot 'get it' using will power. Some teachers say that we cannot go and look for it, but that we have to just let It find us. Others say that there are a few tricks. Some yoga and meditation techniques can indeed make us rediscover 'another' dimension. In this book, we will focus our attention on a few experiments that are developed to make our mind accessible again for this 'other dimension'. These experiments are not the usual meditation techniques or yoga exercises; they simply are pointers to our true nature, which is consciousness.

The first experiment is about turning around our visual attention. In order to do the experiment, we need a sheet of white A4 paper. Then we make a little tunnel by taking that A4 paper and rolling it up so that fits on our right eye. We cover our left eye with our left hand and hold the tunnel with our right hand. It takes two people to do the experiment (see drawing a), but when we are on our own, we use drawing b to look at. Our partner is supposed to go and sit at the other side of that tunnel and put the edge of that other side of the tube to his or her eye.

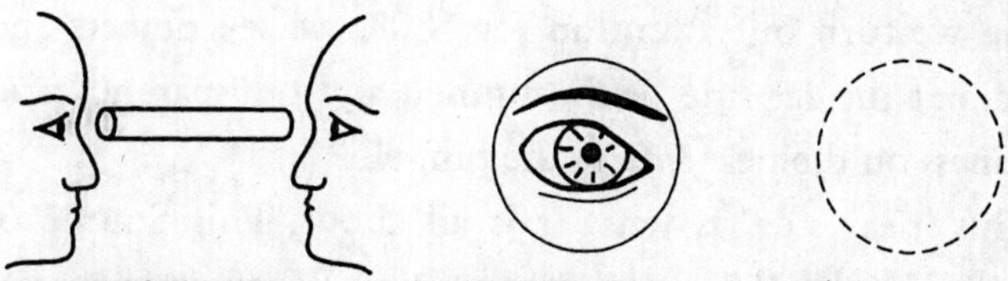

a. outsider's vision b. the other side c. the near side

We start with a very simple question. When we look at our friend's eyeball, do we also see our own eyeball? No, of course not! Let us check it out right now. Believing what others say is of no use here. The eye cannot see itself. So what do we see *on 'our' side*? Let us not think about it but just be clear for one second: what do we notice on our own side of the tunnel? Well, we see… nothing… or is it a nothing filled with awareness? A Light shining from nowhere… Let us have a look again. When we really see clearly, without thinking about it, we see a clear emptiness on our side. We see the eyeball of our friend on the other side of the tunnel (drawing b), and we see pure consciousness on our side of the tunnel (drawing c). It is just a matter of noticing the difference between First Person and second or third person vision. First Person vision corresponds with 'I' or 'me' [the open awareness of the newborn], second person vision corresponds with 'you' [while someone looks you in the face] and third person vision with 'he or she' [while someone looks at your profile].

When we take a closer look in this tunnel, we can notice that we see colours on the other side and transparency on our side. And this is It! There is nothing more to discover, just noticing this aware emptiness on 'our' side is what this experiment is all about. Any child can see this. And we can also notice this, if only we can let go of our concepts and beliefs. While we turn our attention for 180°, we see objects and colours at the far side of the tunnel, and transparency and emptiness on the near side of the tunnel.[19]

This 'near side' is what it is all about. This Source of awareness is what this experiment is about. When we allow this shift of attention, we are turning around our vision through 180 degrees. What we 'get' is a direct contact with our consciousness. Now, what is the point of this experiment? What has this experiment to do with finding our true nature? If we say that in our quest we are going to look for our true essence, for that which is close by, we will have to point our attention to that area at the centre, won't we? That is exactly what we do in this experiment. We take a look at what is close, not at what is at a distance. It is true that it is a bit strange to point at one's eye, but it is the most direct way of getting 'close'. And what do we find here? We do not see anything particular at all, except a light of attention that is shining brightly. Seeing that is a discovery! So that which is so close by, seems to be *pure attention*. This simple awareness is sometimes referred to as a clarity, a transparency. We will use the term 'Consciousness' but many other descriptions are possible. Jan van Ruysbroeck called it 'claerheit' (clearness) and Shakespeare described it as 'our glassy essence'.

THE THIRD EYE

Can I find myself in a mirror?
When looking outwards
you have lost sight to yourself
and your sight remains external.
Turn your look inward.

RAMANA MAHARSHI

There is an ancient phenomenon, better known in the East than in the West, that is described as the 'opening of the third eye.' It is said that this opening of the third eye means that we come suddenly to enjoy an enlightened and unified outlook on life. According to Eastern iconography, this mysterious spot is situated midway between and slightly above the eyebrows. Many stories of the opening of the third eye can be found in the Eastern mystic literature. Here is the story of Ramakrishna, a famous seer who lived in India about a century ago.[20] The turning point in the life of Ramakrishna was when he was approached by a Hindu sage who took a splinter of glass and stuck it between Ramakrishna's eyes and told him to focus on that. The story goes that after a brief period he had a mystical experience that revealed the world in wonder. He saw how to look at the world through one eye, and he got a completely new vision of his life and the world around him. It is said that after allowing this turnabout, Ramakrishna found his true Self.

Many people in the West imagine that this single or third eye is merely figurative. Others suppose it has to do with clairvoyance or with becoming a Hindu fakir. Later it will become clear that the experiments we present in this book have nothing to do with paranormal gifts or extrasensory perceptions. We do not want to see things or phenomena that other people do not see, but quite the opposite: we will learn to see what any child can see! This 'clear seeing' is just a matter of seeing without the belief systems that colour our perceptions. Nothing new will be added: all we do is look without our sunglasses. We could say we go back to the vision of a newborn. Later on, it will become obvious that this opening of our third eye, which we are going to 'experience' in the following experiments, has more to do with a change in what we are looking *out of* than a change in what we are looking at. We do not want to become a mind reader, we do not claim to change the perceptions of the world we are looking at. All we want is to take a fresh look at the one who is looking. Let us do that right now.

We begin with a quite simple question. It concerns the observation of this book we are reading right now. It is a question that can bring us to a discovery which may look childish and quite stunning at the same time. When we are looking at this book, do we see two parts, separated by a vertical border in the middle? In other words, do we see two screens? Science says that we are looking through two little peepholes in our head, called eyes, and that we get a single image through a so-called optical effect. We can check that we have two eyes in medical textbooks on anatomy, so there is no doubt about that, but this is the vision of outsiders. What we are talking about here is the 'vision from inside'. If we ask ourselves again, how many screens we are looking out of, we must confess that there is only one image. It may sound simple or ridiculous, but we see that we are indeed looking through a single screen, and not through two separate screens. In fact, we have never seen through anything else than this big oval window.

When we discover that we see through one screen instead of two eyeballs, we are ready to go one step further. Because in order to reveal our Third Eye, we need an additional step: the turning of our attention by 180 degrees. This turning around of our attention is exactly the same shift we made when we did the tunnel experiment. We should not think that this is going to be the Big Trick; what follows is plain and ordinary, involving no magic whatsoever. But the fact that it is not spectacular does not mean that it is not valuable. By focusing our attention on the inside, on the witness instead of the object, we may come eye-to-eye with the original Subject. This experiment can be utilised by anyone, but that does not mean that everybody will immediately 'see' the Single Eye. To do so, we simply take a look at this book we are reading right now and try to see the difference between this text and the transparent screen from which we look. The former is the object we look at, these black letters on white paper; the latter is the attention that is doing the looking. We can again see that we do not look through those two little windows we call eyes, but out of one large window. Maybe it is too simple to notice it, but this large screen is not a black box but a source of awareness, a wide space of clarity. Even if we close one eye, we can still see the difference between the book in our hands and this awareness 'on our side'; the anatomical details do not matter here any more. Later on we will discover that we can still notice the clarity on this side with *both* eyes closed.

Although this experiment is not spectacular, it can have important consequences for our spiritual search. That will be explained later on. But what is the point of this experiment right now? Seeing this wide space does not change our view of the outside world. What we discover is the difference between an object (in this case: a book), and the Single Eye (the subject, the one who is looking). When the difference between these two becomes clear, it is obvious that the first one is an object over there, at a distance of about 25 cm from our face, and the other one is right here in the very centre of our being. All we did was take a look at the Subject. How can we spend our lives without ever noticing this? It may strike like lightning, or it may approach like the dawn: there is a source of Light that makes it possible to be aware of what we perceive, and all we do in this experiment is take a look at it. All we perceive in our life are *objects*, but this Light is the Seer, the *Subject.* And we have always been looking at our life and our world through this clear lens, through this single TV screen. The Single Eye – that which sees – is borderless, timeless and filled with the entire landscape. Or in other words, the scenery we see changes all the time, but the blank screen remains the same. It is a window through which our world appears to us.

THE ORIGINAL FACE

Everyone likes a mirror,
while not knowing
the true nature of his Face.

RUMI

For the next experiment, we need a mirror. The idea is the same as in the other experiments. The evidence of the senses will be our guiding light, not inherited belief. So we do not accept any pre-packaged idea of what our True Nature is, we try to let go of all our predetermined ideas and address ourselves to the turning of our attention by an angle of precisely 180 degrees. Please do not hesitate to go and stand in front of a mirror to check what we are proposing here. A small hand mirror or a reflection in a window will also do. But thinking about a mirror while reading the text simply will not do. In other words, it is useless just to imagine what the experiment must be like. If there is no mirror at hand right now, wait to continue reading until there is.

The arrow of our attention is always directed at objects and sensations; but what is the bow it is being shot from? This investigation is once again about daring to be our own authority, about seeing the difference between our central reality (the Subject) and our appearance in the mirror (an object). When we stand in front of a mirror, we now try to see the difference between the face in the mirror glass which is our reflection approximately half a metre away, and our transparent face on 'this side'.[21]

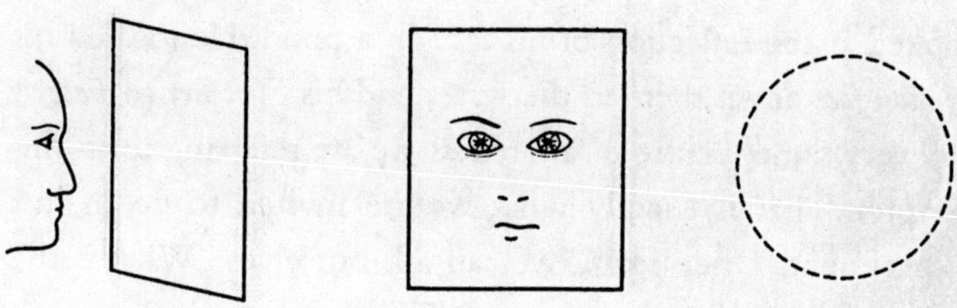

a. third person vision (outsider's vision)   b. second person vision (mirror face)   c. First Person vision (Original Face)

A great trap in this experiment is that we want to see ourselves from the outside, as a third person would see us from a distance (see drawing a). We really have to 'stay on our side', and see what we see. Can we see a difference between these two 'faces'? Can we see the difference between drawing b and drawing c? If we let go of our prejudices, we see on the other side our mirror face (drawing b) and on our side, our naked attention (drawing c), which is pure consciousness. The one over there is an object (our appearance), the one over here is the Subject. Mystics and seers say that this Subject is what we really are. It is the source of the light in our movie, and as such closer to ourselves than our own face. In Zen it is referred to as *the Original Face.*

Maybe we will not believe it right away that a direct contact with our naked Consciousness could be so simple. And although it is not very impressive in the beginning, although it seemed to be no more than a flash of light, we really 'saw' our true Centre. And although we may not realize yet the full consequences of this discovery, this glimpse we had is the naked awareness we were talking about before.

It is said that Tung-Shan (807–869), who became the founder of Soto Zen, saw his [the] Original Face when he looked at the reflection of his face in a pond. He located his *human face* down there in the water and his *First Person Face* at the very same Centre of awareness we are referring to in this chapter. That is exactly what we are invited to do in this experiment. Once again, we can ask ourselves, 'What is the value of seeing this transparency?' The answer to that question will become obvious as soon as we notice the difference between that face on the other side (the object) and the 'face' on this side (the Subject). Let us be our own authority and have another look. We take a look at our mirror again, and check it out for ourselves. Believing is of no use here.

Vision X	**Vision Y**
mirror face	Original Face
two eyes	Single Eye
opaque	transparent

Now, what can we see? There are several differences between our mirror face and our centre of awareness. One difference is that the face on the mirror side has two eyes and the one on our side has only one eye. As we noticed before, we do not look through two little peepholes, but we could say that there is only one big screen on the 'near side'. Actually, there are three eyes: two eyes half a metre away from us, and one large eye on our side of our attention. That is why the Centre of Awareness is called the third eye. This third eye is, of course, not an eyeball in the anatomical sense, but it is a window through which our environment is observed. This window is the Centre of our Being, and will be referred to in this book as naked Consciousness or clear Awareness.

THE SOURCE OF LIGHT

> ***Not one of the 1700 koans of Zen***
> ***has any other purpose***
> ***than to make us see our Original Face.***
>
> **DAITO KOKUSHI**

When we do the mirror experiment, we can say that there is a seeing into the Subject. This Subject is in fact the same as 'naked Consciousness' and is what is referred to as the Original Face in Zen Buddhism. Although from a visual point of view our attention was still filled with our mirror face (drawing b), we – maybe – had a glimpse of our Original Face. Douglas Harding calls this looking back into naked Awareness 'First Person vision'. He says:[22] 'Doesn't it feel absolutely in order, right, true, comfortable? Isn't this entry into our true nature, and haven't we been this all along but we just didn't notice it? Isn't this our

Homecoming?' And what is this aware emptiness like? It is actually a paradox: on the one hand this space is empty, and on the other hand it is *conscious* and filled with everything that appears in it. We could say it is a 'filled emptiness'. It is a light shining brightly. André Breton, leader of the Paris-based Surrealist movement, said:[23] 'I believe that men will long continue to feel the need of following to its source the magical river flowing from their eyes, bathing with the same hallucinatory light and shade both the things that are and the things that are not.'

What is the point of seeing this so-called filled emptiness, this 'looking back' into our own awareness? Isn't it ridiculous to believe that this seeing can bring us spiritual liberation? Can we believe Douglas Harding when he says that this is already It? Is this the same Emptiness all great mystics are talking about? Isn't that approach too simple to be true? Some among us may have expected that seeing this famous Third Eye would be much more difficult. And a far more spectacular experience. And what do we notice? Instead of being a spectacular peak experience, it is rather a valley experience. Although we may think that this 'seeing' is just a little tongue taste of what the great mystics have seen, Douglas Harding says that this *is* already our Original Face. Even if it was only a 'glimpse', it is already It. Having such glimpses of simple awareness may sound marvellous to outsiders, but in fact recognizing this Emptiness is nothing extraordinary at all: this naked awareness is actually our natural state and waking up to it is simply a matter of recognizing it as such. Even when we do not see It, the Infinite is still there! Although such glimpses of naked Awareness are easily disturbed by the noise-making activities of the mind, the Awareness itself is always available. Similar to sunshine being obscured by clouds, we know that the sun is always shining, even when we do not recognize the sunshine directly.

WHO OBSERVES THE OBSERVER?

The nameless is the beginning
of heaven and earth.
The named is the mother
of ten thousand things.

TAO TE CHING

When we ask ourselves who we are, we seem to have numerous identities. When we say, 'I am thinking', the 'I' means our thoughts. When we say, 'I am watching TV', the 'I' means our visual apparatus. When we are writing, we refer to our arms and hands. When we say, 'I am a man' or 'I am a woman', we are referring to our body, when we say, 'I am a philosopher', we are referring to our personality, and so on. But there is another 'I' that is the background of our thoughts and feelings, the essence of our activities and physical characteristics. This 'I' is the Subject. It is the screen *allowing* all these mental images.

As pointed out earlier, it is essential to notice that this Witness is different from our personality; it is even more 'me' than our self-image. The Witness is the Subject, what *is* witnessed are objects. This Subject is the witness *of* our body and mind, but it is not identical to our body and mind. This final witness is the core of our conscious Being and is completely different from the characteristics of our person (although It encompasses this same person). It is in fact the origin of our subjective sense of existence.

As an experiment, we can shut our eyes for a few seconds; we can notice that the visual aspect of the book has disappeared to be replaced by some field of blackness [please, check it out!]. But that change is only visual; all the rest still goes on: thoughts still come and go, feelings arise and replace each other, bodily sensations like pain or pleasure continue to come and go. Sounds appear and disappear. What else can we discover here? Well, the final witness has *not* disappeared during the whole experiment. Even when we would be able to stop all our thoughts, even when there would be absolute silence, this 'I-am-certainty' would still be there. Even when we open our eyes again, the naked awareness itself has not changed; there is only a visual image that has been added to our naked awareness. When someone asks us to try and observe awareness itself, we must admit that we cannot see this background with our eyes. Scientists do not like such a situation; this naked awareness cannot be made an object of scientific observation because it is completely featureless. The final Witness has no spatial dimensions, it cannot be located, it cannot be identified. It is the very means whereby we can observe the sensations that occur in our mind. This impersonal Observer is prior to all sensations; without It there would not even be an experience of existence. Seeing this Single Awareness blows away all the belief systems we ever had, and at the same time we get a perfume of the impersonal Energy where all spiritual traditions are pointing to. It is the single Beingness all conscious creatures share. In other words, there is one Seer in all beings. Hui Hai, the famous Buddhist Zen master, said, 'We do not see with our eyes; we see with our Buddha Nature'.

This Single Eye is the divine Energy that encompasses everything. However, there is a danger in using a word such as 'divine' to describe this Universal Energy. In this book we do not use the word *God* or *Buddha nature* but prefer the terms 'naked Consciousness' or 'impersonal Energy' because these terms do not reduce the Infinite to a finite entity. The word 'God' has been misused in so many ways, especially by those who never even glimpsed the Transparency we are trying to refer to. The Openness we are pointing at in the experiments can not be personalized. [24] And the same is also true for the Source of Light. Personalizing the Impersonal has lead to so many misunderstandings in human history. Once there is clarity about our True Identity, it is obvious that this Source of Light can never be encompassed by a specific religious system. Trying to catch this Infinity into a spiritual system is like trying to put the Pacific Ocean in a cup of tea. The believers of each system are convinced that their cup of tea is the most beautiful one, but those readers who have understood what this book is about will agree that this Transparency has nothing to do with belief systems competing one another. It will be clear that all these paths and organised spiritual systems are only attractive ways to postpone the immediateness of clear Seeing. True Liberation is available right here and right now, and no philosophy or spiritual organisation is needed to see that.

BEYOND DUALISM

How may we perceive our true nature?
That which perceives is our own nature.

HUI-HAI

Since our senses are trained to be pointed outwards, our minds are also set in that same direction and while growing up we have taken the habit of overlooking the one who is looking. We learned to live as a third person, and forgot about the view of the First Person. We forgot about our True Nature and identified with our senses, with what we think we are: our personality.

However, during the witnessing of our True Nature, we may see through the illusion of dualism, although we cannot explain this to anyone else. Once the space-time veil is penetrated through that turnabout of attention we make (e.g. during an awareness-experiment), the distinction between Subject and object falls away. Subject and object become 'one' because the concept of the ego is not standing in the way. It is a bit strange to notice that we can see our true nature exactly during that particular moment when the personal subject has disappeared. Then we [who?] look back into the Single Eye, into the awareness of the One who is looking. And *in* this awareness appears our personality playing the role of its life, as part of the show. The ego imagined itself to be at the centre of our life, but now it shifts back to the periphery, to the world of sensations and objects, thoughts and feelings. At that level, it is allowed to play its role. Seeing this is sometimes referred to as 'Transparent Vision' because we live life from a new perspective now.

This Transparency is in fact so clear that we immediately give up the need to analyse all this. As soon as we start to analyse this Naked Being, we are putting ourselves into the third person position again. This Beingness cannot be examined. We can *imagine* that we take a distance from It and start to analyse it. In fact, we will only have *concepts* about naked being. we will never have an understanding of this Being itself. Usually, we are splitting our world into two things, me (as a person) and something else (a sensation, another person, a concept, a feeling, etc.). Since the Greek philosopher Plato (427–347 BC), such a dualistic approach has always been very popular in western philosophy, and it still is. In dualism, we have a relationship between our 'me' and the rest of the world. Our ego says that these two are separate and that is where dualism begins.

But when we forget about all the concepts of our mind and put in perspective this vision of relationships between our 'me' and the 'not-me', there is a *going beyond all this*. Then we approach the non-dualistic vision. Then, we may recognize the Oneness in everything.

AN OPEN ATTITUDE

There is nothing out there
that needs to be any different,
that needs any change.
What is out there is divine.[25]

TONY PARSONS

Many spiritual teachers say that we have the possibility to discover our Source during moments of silence, and they have developed many techniques to rediscover this Oneness in silence (e.g. during meditation). Still, we must keep in mind that recognizing infinity can also happen when we are active. Later on, we will also see that it is beyond both activity or silence. It is prior to *everything*, prior to any concept and at the same time all-encompassing.

The moments of silence (e.g. during meditation, during an awareness experiment, during a transcendental event) can be – if we can put it that way – a good introduction to rediscover this awareness, but as soon as It is seen once, we realize that it is not dependent on our state of mind. We do not have to practice yoga or meditation to see naked awareness; once we have seen It, we know that the good side of this discovery is that it is available at any time. For instance, the moment we are completely absorbed in one or another action, we can lose ourselves in what happens. When we are absorbed by a particular activity, an intimacy can emerge with this certain action. This seeing, in the sense of watching what happens in our daily life, can become a kind of open-eye meditation, and as such an introduction to what we are referring to in this book.

This seeing seems to be quite difficult to some people but at the same time it is also very simple. The simple side of it is that we do not need any specific skills to see it, the hard part of it is that we have to transcend our personal vision of the world. Usually, we are distracted by the past or the future, we are distracted by our daydreams, our concepts about good and bad, we are hypnotised by our expectations, our goals and our fears. Mentally, we constantly leave the 'here and now as it is' for abstractions, for memories, for fantasies. All this mental chatter keeps us away from what we perceive from Centre, from what happens here and now. Mark McCloskey said:[26]

> There is a gentle, loving, peace-filled silence here and now in this moment. It has always been this way. It is always here. It is right here within you and all around you, a stillness, an apparent void, a seeming nothingness out of which everything arises, exists, and eventually returns.

Recognizing this Silence – and living everyday life from that vision – may leave us with a sense of ordinariness and openness. The inner voice which wants to comment and interfere is in the background now. And although nothing spectacular can be reported, seeing 'This' may leave us with an overwhelming delight, because we appreciate things and people for what they are. Even plain ordinary life is an expression of the divine. And although no permanent state of bliss can be claimed, we see that the infinite is expressing itself *everywhere*.

5

THE POWER OF THE MIND

Man, proud man!
drest in a little brief authority,
most ignorant of what he is most assured,
his glassy essence,
like an angry ape,
plays such fantastic tricks before high heaven,
as makes the angels weep.

SHAKESPEARE

CAN WE DESCRIBE THE TIMELESS?

To awaken suddenly to the fact
that your own Centre is the Buddha,
that there is nothing to be attained
or a single action to be performed,
that is the Supreme Way.

HUANG-PO

We all live according to a thought pattern of linearity, the so-called horizontal time axis: we are told that our life starts with conception, develops to adulthood and ends with death. Society runs on *official* time, ticking away at a steady rhythm. We think of time as something that flows like an endless stream. We stand in the middle of it, in a moment we call the present. Behind, it flows farther and farther away from us, into the past. Ahead, it moves toward us from the future, passing through the present and then into the past. This is referred to as the 'arrow of time' to express its unidirectional quality.

Besides the official time there is also what we call *personal* time. Seen from a subjective point of view, time is experienced as an elastic phenomenon: one minute with the dentist appears longer than one minute during an exciting movie. Our personal experience of time is not a linear time axis, but very elastic. It is more like a swirling mass, where memories are stored, and these memories can come to the surface at any moment. Picking out a souvenir of the memory is in fact an imaginary trip in time. Our mind is capable of escaping from the 'now' by thinking about tomorrow or yesterday. The same principle goes for space: we are always here, but we can think about being somewhere else. Mentally, we can travel in space and time, even if we do not leave our chair: we just use our memory and our imagination. Our memory is a kind of library where we can pick up or bury specific memories, as we wish, and our imagination takes care of the rest.

There are also moments that we seem to live *beyond* time, although we cannot explain this logically because we know that meanwhile the official time keeps on running. For example during the so-called moments of 'pure being' we seem to escape temporarily from the course of time. During such transcendental events, there is nothing but awareness. There is only 'aware Space'. Just as every image of a movie appears 'now', our flow of thoughts also seems to go through the tunnel of the 'now'. During these timeless moments of 'seeing our True Nature' it is suddenly crystal-clear that concepts like 'yesterday' or 'tomorrow' are inventions designed by our mind.. Everything happens now: even the thoughts about our own birth or our own death are now. Even rationally we can understand this: similar to the fact that nobody can escape from 'here', nobody can escape from 'now'. Even when we think about last month, this thought is still now. There simply is no other time than the present, there is no other moment than this moment. We can of course make plans about tomorrow, our intent may be for the future, but our attention is in the present.

Can We Manage Our Thoughts?

When the Self is known,
all illusions vanish.
The veil falls,
and you see clearly.

ASHTAVAKRA GITA

Despite all we discovered in the previous chapters, most seekers will still ask themselves, 'Is there really nothing I can do in order to 'see' Reality, in order to taste the infinite Essence?' We all would like to feel this Essence and at the same time, we understand that feeling It is impossible. We cannot 'get' It and at the same time It cannot abandon us. Even if we choose to ignore It and turn our back, It is closer than our next breath. What do we have to do to 'feel' this Unconditional Love some teachers are talking about? How can we get in contact with this Universal Energy?

The trouble with these questions is not in the answer but in the question. Why do we want to know? Who wants to achieve? The question, 'What do we have to do now?' is a typical question coming from time-related thinking. It comes from the ego, which believes in time and causal connection. It is our 'me' that hopes for Liberation in the future. It is our personality that hopes to be rewarded for its good behaviour. All that can be said is that we do what we do and we get what we get and nobody is sure that these two are related. In other words: what we see is what we get.

Usually we live our life guided by goals, by expectations. We have to deal with problems with our health, with our environment, we have to deal with our fellow people. We plan to have this, we think about changing this situation or that person, we hope to become that, and so on. We accept what is right and avoid what is wrong, or at least we try to do so. As we pointed out before, all of this is possible since we believe in the widely-accepted theory that we have the choice to do good and avoid evil. In other words, we believe that we decide what comes up in our mind, we believe that we decide for ourselves what to do in a given situation. But can we really control our thoughts? If we were able to do so, why don't we choose to always have pleasant and positive thoughts? Suppose we are *not* able to choose our thoughts, we face the next problem: are we responsible for what we do? Or are we just being lived, responding to a series of conditionings, built up by biological systems (e.g. our genetic code, the reflexes of our nervous system, the capacity of our memory), the laws of nature (the mechanisms of our immune system, the drive for procreation, the instincts of survival) and socio-cultural behaviour (e.g. the rules of education, the customs of the society we live in)?

Maybe the joke is that we are supposed to *believe* that we indeed can make choices ourselves. In other words: there is only an *apparent* choice. As we suggested earlier, the concept of being a doer and a decider is only an image passing by. Every idea we have about ourselves is also just a part of the game of life. When unmasking this game, we may gradually realize that life is leading its way anyhow, without our personalities imagining that we are planning it ourselves. Realizing this, we begin to accept that we can live our life as before. In the end, the question of free choice or predestination does not matter any more.

CLEAR SEEING

For everyone that asks,
receives;
and to him that knocks,
It shall be opened.

JESUS

Let us return to what this book is all about: the rediscovery of 'the essence of our being' through clear observation. What follows may appear to be a repetition of what has been told earlier in this book. The repetitions in this book are meant ... ever new pointers to this same No-thing. It is like a cleaning up of the old programmes in our mind. The reflections in this book are like antidotes for all the belief systems and concepts we received when growing up.

We said that during such moments of so-called 'pure being' we feel no longer limited by our body, nor delineated by our skin: we (who?) are open Space. And in that space there is no distance between the 'I' and what we see: there is no more interface between 'me' and 'not-me'. We are, as it were, absorbed into the immediate environment. When discovering this infinity, we are suddenly comfortable in an 'endless Space' where the future is unknown.

Being infinite and unbounded, it may be called our spiritual essence. This pure consciousness is not our self-image; as we said before, our self-image is the role we are playing. When we imagine ourselves to be that role, we are vulnerable: our social mask craves approval, wants to control its life, is afraid of suffering and dying. But when we are not identifying ourselves with a person, when we are not identifying with our hopes or fears, we may find ourselves at home everywhere. Finally, there is no person who gets enlightened, no one who awakens. Nobody, never. Who we truly are has always been awake. And what we think about all this does not really matter that much.

Some teachers say that our ability to 'see clearly' depends on the degree to which we let phenomena unfold naturally in (our) awareness. As we said before, an important hindrance for the ego is our need to always add considerations to the phenomena that we observe: immediately we describe them, think about them. 'Seeing clearly' is in fact a permanent allowing of the uncontrollable [and chaotic] aspect of life. This seeing is not an exercise with a specific goal; it is just to stay with what happens here and now. It is about being open to how the world reveals itself to us: with open arms we let life come to us. Discovering our true nature does not guarantee that all our (personal) problems are solved. Even when the true Nature of our existence has revealed itself, life may still bring us pain and pleasure. Every day life has always new surprises coming up.

What a delight it is to finally see that all is One and to understand that all good and bad are balanced in a perfect way within that Oneness. In fact, since there is no good and bad but in our minds, we finally see that the division into the good guys and the bad guys is just a play of the daydream. But as long as we believe in the daydream, we will have to accept that the good guys will always be balanced by the bad guys and vice versa. That is the rule of universal balance: no North Pole without South Pole. One side cannot exist without the opposite side, and their co-existence compensates perfectly in the end. So, when we get confused by the contradictions and the apparent injustices in this world, we may just keep in mind that all opposite polarities meet in the middle to cancel each other out. As a result, we should not judge too easily, and even be grateful to the bad guys for keeping the balance in equilibrium.

This idea of 'bad keeping the balance for good' is not just true for the 'real' bad guys on television (the drug dealers, the serial killers, the terrorists, the dictators), but also for the 'bad' actions of average people like you and me. The same principle applies if we want to judge our own (or other people's) behaviour: being angry with our partner, getting impatient in a traffic jam, being jealous, unfaithful, disloyal, adulterous, greedy, and so on. Here again, the black phenomena compensate for the white ones. What a relief to see that all we do – be it black or white – is in perfect balance! There can never be a battery with only a positive pole: both the positive and the negative side are essential. There simply is no escape, no matter how hard this is for the judging mind. When we see that positive and negative are two sides of one energy, we automatically stop giving comments. Why should we comment, when everything is as it is? What is the point? What is the goal of judging? As we put in perspective the limited vision of our personal world (vision X), we see that nothing needs to be changed. This doesn't mean that we have to like all and everything. It doesn't mean that everything is perfect. It is simply a matter of seeing that Consciousness has designed it just the way it has to be. Everything we notice: it is all *as it is.*

CAN WE MAKE A CHOICE?

> ***For me, nothing has ever existed;***
> ***all is only an expansion of a thought.***
>
> **H.W.L. POONJA**

When we identify ourselves with the third person (vision X), with the main character of the movie, the so-called daydream does of course seem entirely real: we identify ourselves with our thoughts, and let ourselves be carried away with upcoming fears and desires. When we identify ourselves completely with the main character of the movie, we 'forget' the Original Face and reduce ourselves to a bag with muscles and bones, controlled by a mind. We create a thinker and decider in our heads, and as a result we believe we have a choice to do what we want to do. Our minds not only create a little thinker inside, but also create a virtual reality around us, using our senses and imagination. This so-called daydream, this hypnosis session, has such a high degree of 'looking real' that the day-dreamer does not realize he is playing a role in a daydream. When we are identified with our personality, with its likes and dislikes, with its need for control, we get locked in a rigid mindset. And we wonder why life is going the way it goes. The ego wants to know the hidden plan behind all this.

But is there really a hidden plan behind our life? The ego is allowed to play its role, but now it is seen as a character in a movie. Some spiritual teachers say that the actor just performs his or her role, which is designed by Consciousness. But the actor wants to be the director of the movie, too. Our minds want to know what is going to happen, why things are as they are. The little voice inside wants to be able to say, 'I have done it, and I feel guilty about it' or 'I have decided to do that' or 'I am going to follow that spiritual path'. But can we really know? And can we really decide for ourselves, or do we only *imagine* we can?

The whole issue of being a personality with free will is like a house of cards. It is concept built on concept. Once we see this personality itself is also a concept, the whole house of cards comes tumbling down. However, when we accept that there is no captain in our head, that there is no feeler of emotions in our chest, we can still pretend that we do have a personality with thoughts and emotions, that we do have a free will. It reminds me of the Austrian philosopher Ludwig Wittgenstein (1889–1951) who imagines the leaf falling in the autumn winds, saying to itself, 'Now I'll go this way, now I'll go that way'.

All we can 'do' is pretend as if we have a choice or as if we can do what we want; the result is always the same. The result is that the actor can only act according to his conditionings, according to the reactions of the body-mind machine in the given circumstances. So we are totally free on the one hand and totally programmed on the other. Which means that in the end, it really doesn't matter. Finally we see that this whole issue of choice or predestination is finally not that important (but is only important to our little 'me'). When we identify with our ego, we pretend to be a person, we seem to have a free will. Basically, we think we have a choice and nothing is wrong with that. Indeed, this view is quite interesting from a practical point of view. But this book is not about the practical organization of our life, it is about waking up. It is about waking up from our daydream and in order to let that happen, we may just forget about the practical consequences of our discoveries. Of course, claiming we do not have a personality may sound ridiculous since most of the adult world population lives from that point of view. Those who say they do not have a personality will not be rewarded for claiming that; they will be diagnosed by their physician as having a depersonalisation disorder. The majority of psychiatrists are not familiar with the subject of this book and tend to see such 'stories of spiritual insights' as signs of a serious mental disorder, epecially if people are not able to deal with the consequences in their daily lives. Still, we all feel that we really are a personality, despite what we might discover in the awareness experiments in this book. This personality claims to have a choice, and as a result, our conditioned minds find it hard to accept that we are *being lived*, that everything is happening anyway. In fact, we do not have to imagine any captain inside our head; maybe it is just the way our brains are functioning. Chuck Hillig states:[27]

> You see, if all separation is an illusion, then any further talk about an illusory self having a 'free will' or not would be as useless as arguing about the probable water temperature of a lake mirage out in the desert. Just like there's no real lake out there to be having a water temperature, there's also no real 'separate self' actually

present to be having (or to be not having) a so-called 'free will'.

Especially when the insight of clear seeing appears in the foreground, we recognize the infinity in all manifestation and automatically – without any effort – the desire to identify ourselves with a specific person disappears entirely, except of course for pure practical reasons. So, there is no identification with the main character, no identification with the cameraman, no identification with the director and no identification with the movie. Indeed, when we come Home, there is simply no person to claim anything.

BLACK AND WHITE

Under heaven all can see beauty as beauty
only because there is ugliness.
All can know good as good
because there is evil.

TAO TE CHING

As we pointed out before, there is no good without bad in our minds, but most people do not realize the full consequences of this law. So, let us have a closer look at it. There is this mysterious law of balance that says that to the exact degree of our life being filled with white, we will notice the inverse proportion of black. Realizing this, what is the point of improving our life? For every 'up' there is a 'down' and for every left there is a right. We may believe we have to overcome our bad habits, we may believe that we should be more peaceful, but that is only a lie. A so-called paradise, a perfect world with only white and no black, would immediately be very boring:

white would be the only colour in that paradise, and as a result, would lose its meaning completely. In other words, all the 'good' loses its meaning because it is out of sight, because it is completely gone. It is like writing with white ink on white paper. Our minds would not even recognize such a perfect world (Utopia) if we lived in such a paradise.

It is a cliché, but there are always two sides of a coin. It is all a matter of perspective. What are the practical consequences of really seeing that black and white are always in balance? The major thing is that there is no point in trying to fight the so-called dark sides: not in our own life, not in the lives of other people, not in the life of the planet. Seng-ts'an said: 'If you want to get the plain truth, be not concerned with right and wrong. The conflicts between right and wrong are the sickness of the mind.'

Again: everything is exactly as it is supposed to be. Can we see that? Can the judging mind accept that? What a relief it would be if we could just stop putting all our energy into judging, hoping and resisting. There is simply no point in trying to blow up the white balloons and trying to hide the black ones under the carpet. With the law of balance in mind, we know that the shadow parts of life – the parts we want to throw away – will sooner or later come back, just like a boomerang. It is like trying to get a basket of perfect apples by throwing the bad apples up in the air. In order to get a basket of strictly good apples, we just create the illusion of 'working on a better world' or 'working on a nicer life', but it just does not work that way. Good and bad are not qualities of a person or object *in itself* but concepts in our mind, and as such unreal. So, the bad apples are always coming back to the ground, no matter how high in the air we have been throwing them. That is the force of gravity. The balance is always there, no matter if we see that or not.

Chuck Hillig says:[28] 'After all, doesn't an author love his 'villains' every bit as much as he loves his 'heroes'?' There are so many things in life that just do not seem right, and we feel as if we have to do something about it, even when we realize that all of it is just a daydream. If we feel as if we have to work on it, that is also as it is supposed to be. Then, we are just watching a movie of an actor working on a better world. However, it is an illusion to think that we can really change the scenario of the daydream. It is an illusion to hope we can create a white without at the same time creating a (sometimes hidden) black. Let us see it this way: the white aspects get their meaning as a result of being surrounded by the black ones. We must be grateful (!) to the dark colours for doing their job. We had better leave them for what they are, although the judging mind – the little voice inside – will never like such an idea. The inner voice will say that it is dangerous to state that there is no right without wrong. It sounds as if we are invited to live without any ethical standards.

Many seekers imagine that those who are really living according to the insight 'there is no good without evil' may eventually be turned into asocial citizens, and maybe even cruel human beings. They will criticize this philosophy by saying that it is dangerous to say that it is useless to fight the evil on this planet. Where would that lead to? However, those who really seem to understand what this 'coming Home' is all about do not seem to turn into serial killers afterwards. Most people behave in the same way as before the understanding, and when we remember what we discovered in the awareness experiments – that there is only One Consciousness connecting us all – we immediately see that there is no direct danger when we discover this law of black and white. Most people do not stop helping others. It is rather the opposite, although there are of course no fixed rules.

CLEAR SEEING AS A SOURCE OF COMPASSION

To free people from the idea that they suffer is the greatest compassion.[29]

TONY PARSONS

Most seekers who finally understand that Consciousness is One and that nobody is excluded report that they sense a compassion for 'other' people which they never experienced before. So, in contrast with what a lot of people believe, there is no indifference towards others. To understand this, we have to go back to what we discovered earlier in this book. As we said before, the truth of the matter is that practicing the awareness experiments in this book teaches us that basically *we are all the same*. We may appear to have different physical and mental characteristics from 'other' people, but our essence – aware Consciousness – is One and the same, no matter to what religion or race or nationality we belong. Realizing that despite the differences we are all the same in the eyes of Consciousness, brings us to the core of Buddhist wisdom, namely *compassion* for our fellow people. As soon as we 'see' that the Source of Light is non-dualistic, we also know that any notion of superiority (or for that matter inferiority) is completely ridiculous. We have no reason to feel superior on any level, either in a material or spiritual field. And as we stated before, this understanding can give rise to a total acceptance of what is. There is always this divine balance, although it is not always easy to see this balance in everyday life.

It is true that it is hard to accept that good and bad are in balance, especially when we look at the news on television. It sounds as if we don't care any more. We all have a habit of labelling one kind of behaviour as wrong and another as right.

Although we can 'see' that our opinions are relative (someone else may have a different view on the same subject), we take our opinions seriously as long as we believe in vision X. Although we have to admit that those images of 'good' and 'bad' are no more than concepts passing by in our mind, we still find it difficult to accept that in the end all is in a perfect balance, even when we know that notions and opinions can never touch the simplicity and neutrality of this blank canvas.

Those who see all this with clarity know that in the end we are arguing about a daydream. What is the point, anyway? While we are sitting in a movie, do we say that the bad guy is really bad and the good guy is really good? Both are just actors, paid to play their role, that's all. They are just doing what Consciousness is telling them to do. Who are we to judge them? The Light that makes our movie visible does not care if someone is playing the good guy or the bad guy. Consciousness does not care. And Consciousness has no preferences to whether our movie is a romantic movie or a horror movie. In fact, Consciousness is just the final Witness of what happens, without judging or planning. Does the Light in the movie theatre judge the behaviour of the actors? This Light, this final Witness is a sort of empty calmness that allows everything that is. It witnesses both pain and joy, both serenity and stress, without any preferences or comments. And that witnessing is what we really are: totally constant, still and calm, allowing everything. There is simply no agenda in this witness, no consideration about right or wrong, no consideration about who is the good guy and who is the bad guy. The compassion that flows from this understanding is absolutely unconditional.

6

CAN THIS SEEING BE PRACTISED?

You need not acquire anything

to realize this.

You need only subtract beliefs,

Which obscure your living as this radiant presence,

as love itself…

It is immediately accessible to you,

Even as you read these words.[30]

CATHERINE INGRAM

AVOIDING THE VOID

When an onion is peeled continually
all skin goes away and no substance is left.
Similarly on analysing the ego
it is found to be no entity.

RAMAKRISHNA

Generally we believe our minds are somewhere in our heads, separated from the world. Most of us seem to experience ourselves to be located somewhere within that image made up by the mind. We have created our own image of reality and have quite naturally put ourselves at the centre of this image. We simply locked ourselves up in the middle of an imaginary prison. The whole world we have constructed is imagined around a central point, the centre of our perception. We think that the central point of our visual experience is somewhere in the middle of the head. As a result, we see ourselves to be somewhere behind the eyes. We imagine ourselves to be some spirit that lives in the head and looks at the world through two windows, through two peepholes called eyes. This is where we quite naturally place ourselves within our image of reality. Since the brain is also located in the middle of the head, somewhere behind our eyes, it is assumed that Consciousness is somehow located in the brain. But on closer inspection we are unable to find a 'central container' in our head. Consciousness is the container of our world, but that does not mean that Consciousness is contained within the brain [the Consciousness we are talking about here is much wider than the consciousness medical scientists are referring to: the latter is just a particular part of the first].

We discovered in the experiments, what many seekers have already experienced in meditation or transcendental events: that we are not limited to this body-mind machine. We may find that what we really are is conscious Space, which is infinite, edgeless and open to *what is*. In other words: we recognize a 'bigger' version of me. We discover that besides the little me (the concept of being a body) there is also a 'big me' which is the Witness of all this. A Subject, always ready to be filled up by objects. So, those among us who have 'seen' clear Awareness can confirm that Consciousness is not located in our head. Consciousness is not hidden somewhere, it is *everywhere*. As a result, mystics say, 'There is only one Consciousness'. Of course, at the level of the senses, we all have a private consciousness because we all see an individual and unique movie. However, the Consciousness that witnesses all this is not private but infinite. This infinite Consciousness is always fully present in its absolute totality, right here and right now – even when we do not recognize It as such.

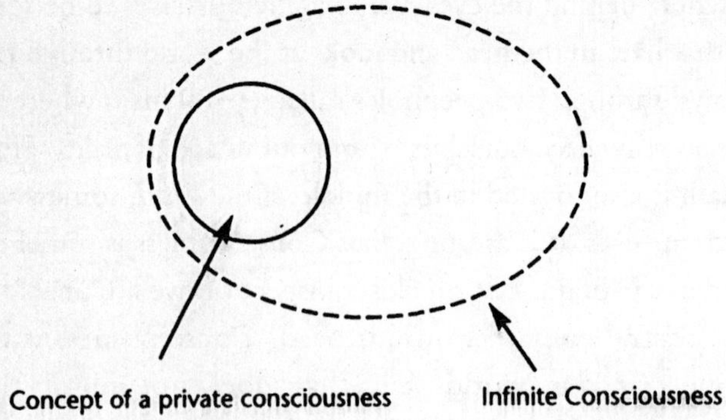

In short, what we are experiencing now is already an expression of the Infinite! No matter what activities appear to be happening in our movie, the fundamental truth beneath it all is the Screen that is supporting all of the dramas being played out. It is like One big Screen on which billions of movies are played simultaneously.

Although it is clear that such 'big' Consciousness must be all pervading and all encompassing, some people still feel uncomfortable by seeing 'This'. Realizing that we may appear to have separate bodies and individual senses and at the same time One Consciousness is like the light bulb discovering electricity. It puts our personal importance in perspective, and most philosophers in the West have a strong resistance to that idea. That is why this non-dualistic vision will never be very popular. And most seekers are very attached to their ego, both in the East and in the West. Some people do not want to see this Void because their egos are afraid of disappearing. This fear of the emptiness (e.g. felt when trying an awareness experiment), is immediately repressed; people avoid such an upcoming feeling of discomfort as soon as it surfaces. This fear of the unknown may feel like dying. However, nothing really dies, only names and concepts appear and disappear. Those who really see this will confirm that in fact there is no personality that dies, because the personality is just a concept. What remains is this universal Energy, this Light which is always shining brightly.

LIBERATION IS NOT A DEAL

> *The recognition of the fundamental, essential nature*
> *of Reality*
> *is the source of our greatest satisfaction and deepest*
> *fulfilment.*[31]
>
> **METTA ZETTY**

Now, what do we have to do about all this? What matters in our quest for the ultimate and all-encompassing truth is recognizing this, not doing something about it. It is said that we are already what we are looking for. So, there is nothing to do, and nothing to exclude. Liberation or 'waking up' is not the attainment of anything new, it is not the discovery of a higher state of mind, it is just a waking up to what we are. So it is not about changing ourselves: the actor can continue to play his role, just as before. It is simply a rediscovery of the essential truth about what actually is: we think we are a movie star, but we forget that our bigger Me is the Light. The movie star is just one of the images appearing on the Screen.

When we see this, we simply view every person as an extension of Consciousness, and we embrace what is-as-it-is. No judgement, no labelling, no opinion about it, and no preference for 'this' to 'that'. When we stop talking to ourselves, when we cease categorizing all we perceive, we see that all this labelling is an abstraction. What is the relevance of giving a description of a perception, except that it is useful for communication? Is saying the word 'book' the same as the book we are holding in our hands right now? Is the sound 'book' ever coming close to it? Is what our fingers feel coming close to the 'real' book? Is what we are reading the ultimate reality? Finally we see that all our experiences are subjective. And we realize we are creating our own little world with our own mind and that the idea of an objective 'outside world' is based on agreement but not on perception. Of course, we have built a 'real world' in our minds for practical reasons, using language and symbols, but that does not change the fact that all we perceive is coloured by our own body-mind machine. And that even that body-mind machine is part of the game. Ideas and concepts only exist in our minds: we can never put our finger on an idea or a concept. That is why the physical world is referred to as conceptual, as an illusion. A dream world – a virtual reality – which is created and destroyed all the time. That is the magic of the daydream we think we live in. Tony Parsons writes:[32]

> The life story that has apparently happened is uniquely and exactly appropriate for each awakening. All is just as it should be, right now. Not because it is a potential for something better, but simply because all that is, is divine expression.

This divine manifestation expresses itself through a daydream which looks personal. This 'private' daydream needs a white screen, an empty Space, and that Space is *not* private. The story of our life seems to happen in a Space which is impersonal. All the appearances [all these illusions of the daydream] come and go into this Space which Itself does not change. It looks like an eternal cycle of creation and destruction. What comes must change, must go. As long as we believe in the concept of time, this wheel will never stop spinning.[33]

OUR NATURAL STATE

> ***All efforts to be rid of the ego***
> ***merely reinforce the sense of identification with it.***[34]
>
> **NATHAN GILL**

We have been referring to 'clear awareness' and 'transparent vision', but what is it really all about? Although this looking back into our naked consciousness might seem to be a new vision, it has been at the heart of almost every testimony to awakening throughout mystical literature. It is what has been called the 'natural state' which can be directly seen and realized as soon as we cease to pay attention to the passing clouds and let ourselves be enlightened by the direct sunlight. We finally see that what we really are is like the blue sky which the clouds pass through. This does not imply that we have to see ourselves as a blue sky or that we are invited to imagine our centre as a white canvas; the empty sky or the white screen are metaphors for our transparency, for our emptiness. What we really are at centre is not a blue sky or a movie screen in the sense of a state of mind or a special sensation. It is the Light that makes our movie visible, and as such it is completely beyond words or thoughts.

Although the reflections in this book are designed to help us rediscover the Source of light in the images of our life, we will find out that 'Realisation' does not emerge through personal effort, that finding our True Nature is not a direct result of contemplation or belief. Later we will confirm that Liberation cannot be the result of our personal attempts to make our lives more spiritual but something that happens when it is allowed to appear. When we witness the ever changing flow of mental images we may be absorbed by the One who is looking. In this so-called Transparent Vision there is no point of view about anything, but rather a state of no-judgement. There is seeing beyond belief, and things are just as they are. As soon as our mind polarizes and says, 'I think that things are like this', the opposite arises simultaneously and is given reality. When we transcend our senses, we can see that all manifestation, positive or negative, arises out of this Awareness, out of this one Source. Seers and mystics say that dualism is transcended. Then, nothing is left except awareness. But again: a hidden trap in all of this is that we think, 'I am Awareness', while we still act from the thinking ego, while we still try to understand the transparency using conceptual knowledge. We try to think our way out of this problem, but 'seeing' is not a matter of thinking. Our true nature is not an object, not something that can be perceived by the five senses or that can be conceived through paranormal capacities. That is why we are never able to find this Awareness in this book: words will always fail to describe this Openness.

THE ETERNAL INVITATION

> ***Let subject and object be so one***
> ***that the wind cannot pass between them.***
>
> **WU-MEN**

The so-called timeless moments of 'naked Beingness' can appear when doing meditation or a seeing experiment, but can also appear without any specific practice. With time, one becomes less and less dependent on techniques and one is more and more 'seeing' during everyday situations. But we expect the invitation to appear in the extraordinary and not in the ordinary. We all want an invitation to see the infinite in a peak-experience of bliss. However, if the infinite consciousness is all-encompassing, it must be equally available in anger, in fear. We all want to recognize Oneness in the silence of meditation or in the beauty of the sunset, but It must also be there in pain, boredom, stress and problems.

Although seeing this Space can happen in any situation and at any time, it seems more likely that we can access the field of pure awareness when we are not disturbed by the turbulence of everyday activities. This is especially true in the beginning. For example, spending time in nature can enable us to sense the harmonious interaction of all the elements and forces of life. Whether it be a forest, a mountain river, a seashore or the stars at night, we can witness the effortless ease and carefree harmony nature shows us. This direct connection with nature's harmony may lead to a discovery of our impersonal Beingness. Another way of discovering the harmony of the natural forces is by letting ourselves be overwhelmed by sexual energy: this force is a very rich expression of the impersonal power of creation itself. This will be discussed in future chapters.

This Beingness shown by the natural forces is in fact the seed of recognizing our natural state. These are moments where one acts without thinking, without planning, without comparing. All belief systems are put in perspective. One lives without any goals, without any expectations. Similar to the automatic gearbox of a car, the making of decisions occurs without any interference of an imagined doer or thinker. In other words: everything seems to happen spontaneously, naturally, and the magic is that we do not realize it! The little thinker in our head who always has commentaries, has all of a sudden been silenced, and without realizing it, our captain in his control room has disappeared. Tony Parsons writes:[35]

> When I know who I am I discover that I am not existence, I am the presence which allows existence to be... It is the open secret which reveals itself in every part of our lives. No effort, path of purification, process or teaching of any kind can take us there.

Once we have discovered the transparency, we can allow presence everywhere, and all the books (including this one) and all the meditation techniques (including the experiments in this book) become superfluous. These moments of simply being may emerge while walking in the woods, when watching the flames of a fire, admiring the clouds in the sky, swimming in the sea, when we are dancing, making love, driving on the highway, enjoying a glass of wine, or when we are completely absorbed by a work of art.

When we look at art that points to the ultimate, that reveals the infinite within us, it simply takes our breath away. Automatically, we remember that there must be more to reality than we thought. It is not that we go into another dimension, we rather are absorbed in 'that which is beyond dimensions'. Some works of art (it may be a painting, a sculpture, a poem, a piece of music or whatever) can indeed call us beyond our concepts about the world. They take us *beyond ourselves*. Such works point to a transpersonal space where the Original Face shines in Its full glory. In a glimpse, we are confronted with the deepest we can feel, the highest we can imagine: we transcend ourselves and get a taste of our most profound Ground. This is art in one of its most original and highest meanings: it works like a catalyst which uncovers our True Identity. All these images are in fact pointers to the imageless and can bring to the surface the recognition of our infinite nature.

Some works of art reflect the deepest longings of the human heart as it searches for the infinite in a very particular way. They celebrate unconditional love, they evoke both the agony and ecstasy of yearning after our birthright. Some works of art can be a direct invitation to rediscover the infinite aspect of our existence. Both contemporary works of abstract art (e.g. Kazimir Malevich[36], Barnett Newman[37], Mark Rothko[38], Yves Klein[39], Ad Reinhardt[40], Anish Kapoor[41]) as well as ancient Hindu and Buddhist yantras (abstract meditation images used in the Tantric tradition[42]) are sometimes like mirrors that reflect the desperate search for our most intimate self. Their whisper may be urgent, reflecting the desire to transcend our human conditionings. All these 'mirrors' can be arrows penetrating to the deepest layers of our infinite nature, silently nurturing an affinity for the real Centre. They may become catalysts in our longing to come Home.

Listening to the Silence

> *Only when you drink*
> *from the river of silence*
> *will you really sing.*[43]
>
> **Kahlil Gibran**

We said that every activity can be an opportunity to allow Presence, which means that there are no rules or limitations with respect to the situation in which we can see our true nature. Everybody is ready for Liberation. It is not exclusive for those who are in a special state. Being without concepts is not dependent on anything. Liberation is not exclusive for special people or for special situations. That is why we can say that the approach in this book is democratic: nobody is excluded, and it is available at any time. In other words: *It* is not a collector's item. So, it is rather a matter of letting go than a matter of gaining. Our infinite nature can be revealed in any situation. Any sense can be a 'tool' to rediscover It: seeing, touching, hearing and so on. In this chapter, we will discuss the latter. For example when listening to music, we may ask where the sound is. Maybe we can see that the sound is taking place within awareness, just as the other sensations float in this same awareness. We can notice that the sound is bordered on every side by a receptive silence. This is the aware silence that allows that particular sound to be heard. And when that sound stops, we may 'hear' the silence right where the sound was.

When we 'listen' to that silence, we can see that the silence is not just in this awareness, it *is* this awareness. Awareness and silence are interconnected, they are one. When we completely let go of self-centred thinking, our notion of space and time disappears, and we see a stillness in which the universe appears. This pure Silence is without divisions, and everything arises out of it, and disappears back into it. It is clear, infinite Consciousness, and it is what we are built of.

When we hear a small, distant sound like a bird song or a car engine in the street, we notice that these sounds also arise out of that silence and 'fall back' into it. It is this silent awareness that allows these sounds to be heard. Hearing this silence is sometimes referred to as 'real hearing'. The same is true when we are totally absorbed by music. For example, when we are not anticipating the sounds we expect, we just let the music flow. Then our ego may disappear and we become one with the listening: we actually 'become' the music. In fact, we do not hear music with our ears, but we seem to feel it with our whole body; the concept of identifying with our body evaporates… The sense of hearing is put aside; it is as if there is no interface any more between our 'me' and the music we think we listen to: the music goes right through us, it *replaces* us. Suddenly, we realize that we are not *in* that body-mind machine which is hearing some music that is at a distance. Suddenly, the separation is gone: we realize that the music does not play for us, it plays *within* us. For example, when we are listening to piano music, we discover (afterwards) that there was no listener. This is also reported by musicians themselves. Many musicians – especially jazz players – report that most unexpectedly they are really losing themselves. When the identification with the body-mind machine has dropped completely, we see that the primordial truth is the music; the relative truth is the 'I and the piano'. As a Zen Master put it, 'When I heard the sound of the bell ringing, there was no I, and no bell, just the ringing'. There is not a person listening on the one hand and the music on the other hand. No inside and no outside, no subject and no object – just immediate experience itself.

How far do we have to search?

Many have searched for light and truth,
but only out there where they are not.
In the end they go so far away,
that they never return to find their way inside.
Neither have they found the truth,
for the truth is their ground, not outside.

ECKHART

Once we have tasted the perfume of naked Consciousness, we see clearly what this book is about. One glimpse of 'It' is more effective than all the words in this book. But when the transcendental event is over, we may be disappointed. We feel as if we lost it. To many seekers, there seems to be a give and take between vision X (common sense) and vision Y (seeing the infinite everywhere). Some among us imagine there is an ebb and flow between being conscious of our True Nature, and overlooking it. It really looks like that in the beginning, and many seekers get trapped in this idea. They think they have lost the Source, and do everything to get it back again. They don't realize that the Source is right here, nearer than our breathing, nearer than our mind. When we do look here (as we did in the seeing experiments), we see that this Awareness *never* disappears because it is beyond our concept of time. When Awareness is seen, we discover that what we are looking for can never escape. It can never escape because it is everywhere. This naked Consciousness is always present, no matter if we think we see it or not. Even when the sky is clouded, the sun is shining.

Since most of us do not feel that we really have discovered our True Nature, the following questions arise: what prevents us from seeing this original essence all the time? What clouds are in front of the sunshine? Which belief systems have to be taken out of the way in order to see this field of Consciousness? Why are we not able to take off our sunglasses? How can we not see That which is always there? How can we ever *not* be what we *are*? Realizing that the infinite can never disappear, we understand that in fact there is *nothing* that can prevent us from seeing It.

In mystical literature we read about people who have 'woken up' into a larger, broader and deeper understanding of the fundamental nature of reality. Those who have experienced a 'clear seeing' into the Essence of human existence are indeed a source of inspiration. They want to share with us the 'Essential' and want to guide us toward our own innate recognition and realisation of who we are. They say that true Liberation is available for everyone who dares to look. But they also insist that this will only happen if our vision is broad enough to encompass harmony as well as contradiction, the profane as well as the spiritual, the obvious as well as the paradoxical. We have to put in perspective the powers of the mind and let all personal ambitions go. In other words: we have to take off our sunglasses, and simply 'see'. But it doesn't seem to be that simple. Religious and spiritual literature often suggests that true salvation is only accessible to special people, and that finding this awakening means that we will be above all human shortcomings, that we will be in an almost divine state where all problems are dissolved. Often it suggests that only saints, seers or avatars are perfect enough to see the Truth. All these stories are not very encouraging for the average seeker. As our human shortcomings remind us daily that we are far from perfect, we must conclude that this awakening is not for normal people like you and me. It suggests strongly that we still have a long way to go before we can reach this state of perfection. By searching to find the Essence of our human existence, many so-called spiritual seekers are usually interested in growth, in their betterment. They hope to grow in their spiritual evolution by reading the right books, doing the right exercises or living according to the rules of a specific tradition. The question is, is this really necessary? Do we really have to practice meditation in order to find our true nature? Do we have to pray in order to become ready for a higher spiritual level? Do we have to devote our life to a holy person or a holy scripture to become worthy? Is it essential to become a better person in order to be able to discover inner peace? Is it logical to think that Liberation is only for those who behave according to the rules of a specific tradition, when we know that what we are looking for is universal? How can one seeker be better than another one if the Truth we are seeking is all-encompassing? How can one thing be worthy and another not? How can one person be excluded if this quest is about non-dualism?

It is important to answer the above questions if we really want to get to the bottom of this investigation. What a relief it would be if we realize that we are OK as we are right now, and that there is no reason to improve ourselves, that we do not need any therapy or discipline to find our inner Source of fulfilment, that we do not have to become saints or mystics to discover this naked awareness. Tony Parsons is famous for not making any compromise in this issue.[44] He writes:[45]

> Doctrines, processes and progressive paths which seek enlightenment only exacerbate the problem they address by reinforcing the idea that the self can find something that it presumes it has lost. It is that very effort, that investment in self-identity that continuously recreates the illusion of separation from oneness. This is the veil that we believe exists. It is the dream of individuality.

The basic message of most religions is that something is wrong with the world, and with the people living in it. Some pretend to know what is wrong and what to do about it. The problem with following a spiritual path is that it can give us the impression that 'we are not there yet'. It informs us that we must go on a certain road before we can reach the promised salvation. The top of the mountain seems so far away and we are expected to work hard to reach the top. The problem with maps and ground plans is that they suggest we have to travel a specific way. Often the trap with spiritual organizations is that they give us the impression that we are far away from our goal; that *they* will give us the rules of how to get there, and that they are the only ones who know the secret way to the top.

7

A NEW PERSPECTIVE

Stop all delays, all seeking and all striving.
Put down your concepts, ideas and beliefs.
For one instant be still and directly encounter
the silent unknown core of your being.
In that instant, Freedom will embrace you
and reveal the Awakening you are.[46]

ADYASHANTI

The Love Song of the Wave to the Ocean

If I'm 'all there is',
then I'm everything
and I'm everywhere.[47]

Chuck Hillig

It is one thing to see our true nature, but we may continue to think that it takes special attention to be aware of it through everyday activities. As we said earlier, discovering our Transparency can happen in one second, but living from it every day may take repeated attention – not to discover something new, but just to unmask the mental or emotional habits that seem to cover this Transparency. Similar to a computer system which is handicapped by old programmes and irrelevant data, our nervous system is obscured by all the belief systems it has built layer after layer. All these mental constructions cover up the underlying Transparency, which never really disappeared. The reflections in this book can be interesting catalysts to delete these old programmes.

This still sounds as if we are going to achieve a higher state somewhere *in the future*. What would it be like if we were to recognize naked awareness *within the present moment*? Right now, while reading these words. How would life unfold if we allowed this to be the background for everything that exists? If we suppose that the present moment is infinite, if we imagine that anything we can experience through our mind and senses is only a limited part of who we are, how would this influence our way of looking at the world? What would it be like if all this were not a matter of imagination, but of reality? How would that influence our sense of identity? If we imagine that the so-called reality is one Unity, how would this understanding affect the way we live our life? How would this recognition of Oneness affect the way we deal with other people? Just seeing that all human beings share this One Consciousness, how would that influence our behaviour? How would this recognition of the aware Silence affect the way we deal with the problems in today's society? Being aware of this Openness may be an exciting starting-point to living our life in a smooth and natural way. As the mind surrenders to this Awareness, there is an awakening to the fullness of who we really are. Already being acquainted with this Unity and once having 'tasted' the transparency within us, we let the images on our screen appear and disappear until the Background reveals itself spontaneously. This shift in perception may reveal a vision that is already there but which has not been recognized yet. So in the end, there is nothing to gain and nothing to lose: all is just happening automatically. Tony Parsons says:[48]

> The dream we are living has absolutely no purpose other than our awakening from it. That awakening emerges outside of the dream, outside of time, and is completely beyond the grasp of individual effort, path, process or belief.

In the beginning it may look like a struggle we go through between our 'naked being' on the one hand and the identification with the personality on the other hand. Our life still seems to continue to balance between transparency and limitation, between openness and contraction, between First Person vision and third person vision. As we said before, many teachers say that depending on our attention, we can focus on our personality and the life it is living, or our attention can be filled with the 'impersonal dimension'. In the first case, we identify with our body and mind and live as a person in the world. When we think we are no longer seeing the infinite in and around us, we 'retract' back to the separate person. We identify ourselves with this illusion bordered by the limits of our body: we believe that we are limited to this person that is sitting here reading this book. In other words, we reintroduce our limited sense of self. In the second 'situation' we see the dream of the person we have taken ourselves to be and discover the Consciousness 'behind' our life. We see there is one universal Energy, penetrating all and encompassing everything.

Instead of thinking that we live in the world, we see (or better, 'it is seen') that the world happens *in us*. In other words, we realize that our life appears in Consciousness. When we put all our belief systems in perspective, we strip Awareness naked and the treasure which is beyond space and time is revealed. At the level of such Transparent Vision, we are unlimited, boundless, unborn and undying. Still we may feel that we are hypnotized again and again by the belief that we are separate human beings, that we are one of those six billion human beings on this earth. How can we reconcile this feeling of separation with the above mentioned recognition of infinity? It is said that we are human beings, but what does that word really mean? The 'human' part is made up of our feeling of separation, whereas the 'being' part is the feeling of oneness. The first one is our personality, the second one is our Centre of Oneness; both are two sides of one reality, as the wave and the ocean are both manifestations of the element water. In other words, we are all different in the way we express awareness, but the Awareness itself is One. So there is both diversity and equivalence. The same concept can also be recognized in some Japanese Zen Gardens.[49] The human part is expressed by the rocks (vertical element), the Being part is symbolised by the sand (the horizontal element). The human part is based on the feeling of being separate (vision X), the Being part relates to our sense of being infinite Awareness (vision Y). Just as the waves and the Ocean are one entity, the rocks and the sand are the symbols of one universal Energy: the rocks are – just like sand-castles on a sandy beach – *extensions* of the sand. So the rocks and the sand seem to be separate, but in essence they are One.

Keeping both options in mind, we 'see' we are extensions of this same universal Energy, and as such infinity in disguise. We see that we are both wave and ocean simultaneously, we recognize that we are form and formlessness simultaneously. Rather than being just another wave in the ocean, we see that our Essence is the ocean itself. This is called the love song of the wave to the ocean: the conversation between individuality and universality.

THE ILLUSION OF PERCEPTION

You are the deep innerness of all things,
the last word that can ever be spoken.
To each of us you reveal yourselves differently:
to the ship as coastline, to the shore as ship.

RUMI

Earlier we discovered that when we take this book in our hands, we cannot state if we actually feel the paper or if we just notice what is going on in our fingertips. What happens from a medical point of view, is a transmission of signals from the receptors in our skin to the central nervous system; then it goes up the spinal cord until it reaches the brain. A specific electric current evokes a chemical reaction in the nerve cells of the cerebral cortex, which corresponds to a specific sensation of our fingertip touching the paper of this book.

We see objects and persons because we build a mental image of them in our mind: that is simply the way our nervous system is functioning. When we watch an object, that mental image in our mind depends on the position of our eyes relative to that object; furthermore, it is influenced by the way our mind integrates all these impulses to one specific image. Additionally, this mental image is shaped by experiences from the past and compared with current experiences; it is also coloured by our expectations and beliefs. Immanuel Kant said: 'External things, namely matter, are in all their configurations and alternations nothing but mere appearances, that is, representations in us, of the reality of which we are conscious.'

The so-called real world (the planet we think we are all living on, all these continents and oceans, all these people living on it) is sometimes referred to as an illusion, as a daydream, because it has no separate identity apart from our mind. Seeing this illusion, recognizing the hypnosis of the daydream is similar to waking up from a dream in the middle of the night: as long as we believe in it, it looks real. That is the magic trick of our mind: we create a world around us, and as we believe in it, every aspect of it is true. In other words, we create our own (virtual) reality, and whether that concerns cars and houses, or our body and its desires, it does not matter. We can create (and destroy again) whatever we like. All our beliefs, be it in souls and spirits or in past lives, it looks all as real as can be *for each individual who believes in it*. They are all products of the mind. They look real because we have all created them ourselves, and nothing is wrong with doing so. That is the way our mind is working. Seers and mystics sometimes state that discovering the illusory aspect of our world is similar to waking up from a dream at night. When we are dreaming during our sleep, everything we see or feel in the dream looks real. These images are all produced by the mind. But that cannot be proved or falsified. Even if something impossible happened in the dream, our mind reconciles itself to the vision of the dream. In other words, the dream as a dream does not permit us to doubt its reality. In exactly the same way, we are unable to doubt the reality of the so-called real world of our wakeful experience. As long as we are daydreaming, it looks real. Both the world of wakeful experience and the dream world are but creations of the mind. Suppose we feel thirsty in a dream, the illusory drinking of illusory water can quench our illusory thirst, but all of this is not illusory to us as long as we do not realize that the dream itself is illusory. And we could draw a similar scenario for the so-called real world: does the world exist by itself? Is the universe ever seen without the aid of the mind? Many spiritual teachers say that when we wake up from the daydream, we realize the relativity of its existence, and we can ask ourselves again, 'Is it the outside world that says that it is real, or are we just pretending it is real?' This reminds us of the following Zen story.

> Two Zen monks were arguing about a flag.
> One monk said: 'The flag is moving.'
> The other monk said: 'The wind is moving.'
> The sixth patriarch happened to pass by, and said:
> 'Not the wind, not the flag; mind is moving.'

In fact, all the knowledge we have to construct the so-called real world is only real *while we are awake*: it vanishes immediately when we fall asleep. But even right now, while we are awake and reading the words, is it this book that says, 'I am real', or is it our mind that says so? We can look at this book, touch it, read it, and still we may wonder if it is really real... All we 'have' are but images in our mind.

The famous Indian story of the rope and the snake illustrates this idea. A man is walking through the forest and suddenly he thinks he sees a snake lying in the grass right in front of him. He is terrified (his brother died after a snake bite, six months ago) and wants to run away until he takes a second look. He watches carefully and realizes that the snake is not a snake but a rope. He realizes that he lived in a virtual world, built up by his own fears. What happens? His fear disappears – although nothing has really changed: the rope is still there – and the man goes on his way, smiling.

AS REAL AS IN THE MOVIES

Apart from thoughts,
there is no independent entity
called the world.

RAMANA MAHARSHI

When we see ourselves as a spectator of our own life, it is as if we are sitting in a movie theatre watching the movie entitled 'Autobiography of Myself'. When we recognize the Light in the images on the screen, we see that the role we are playing is indeed just a role. Then we can see that our film is mere illusion. That it is a daydream that appears in the consciousness field, a series of pictures that appear on a blank screen.

This is only a first step. We also realize that in the so-called daydream, we do not perceive what we perceive, but what our mind adds to the perception. As we said before, the mind uses memory, fantasy and abstraction in order to create a virtual personality that is living in a virtual world. In doing so, we build up our life starting from a personal perceiver, influenced by education, religion, the rules of society, 'personal' experiences, and so on. As a result, we also create a virtual world that surrounds this virtual person, using the same mechanisms (memory, fantasy and abstraction). But when all those ideas, beliefs, convictions, opinions, etc. are unmasked as concepts of the mind, we realize that actually we can have a much broader perception of what is going on. When we realize that the events in the daydream are not real, we can recognize that the *dreamer* is also an illusion.

Just as the dreamer is a figure of the dream (while we are sleeping), the daydreamer is a figure of the daydream (while we are awake): the 'me' during the day (the person who pretends to be walking around on this planet) is also a mental construction. We identify ourselves with this body-mind machine that is continually responding from a series of conditioned belief systems. As pointed out before, we create for ourselves (and for others) a series of personal characteristics and qualities like guilt, egocentrism, sin, heroism and so on. We put all our characteristics together in one box, and say, 'This is what I feel', and 'This is what I think', and 'That is what I am like'. Finally we put all of our so-called characteristics together in one box and we say, 'This is *what I am'*, but can we really do that? Is this what we really are, a collection of thoughts, feelings and perceptions? In fact, the identification with our major characteristics is itself no more than a fleeting image. And it is a trick of our memory that makes it look 'lasting' although it has no permanent reality.

The moment the Witness is rediscovered, is a magical moment. It may happen during a transcendental event, or we may just wake up one morning and say, 'Of course, it is so obvious!' Then it is suddenly 'seen' that our personality – that which we always thought we were – is something which can be observed! As we discovered in earlier chapters, it is a 'thing' (a concept, an idea) among other things that can be noticed. It is just an image passing by on the screen. When we see that what we really are is the witnessing process of all this, we realize we are not limited to this body-mind machine which is reading this text right now. The true centre is Consciousness, not our self-image. And this witnessing quality has never left us! Isn't it amazing to see – to really see – that the 'light' which looks through our eyes now, is the same light when we were fifteen years old, and will be the same light when we are fifty or seventy or ninety years old? This Light, this Consciousness, is timeless, and changeless. Yes, it is always there, whether we recognize it or not.

Eternity is now

The future and past
are thoughts in the minds of the characters
that you – Consciousness are playing now.[50]

NATHAN GILL

When we are identified with the mind, we live through memory and anticipation. We are trapped in our own web of time. We live in a *conceptual* world, hypnotized by the past and the future. Why is that? Well, believing in time is the favourite game of the ego. What is so attractive about the past, then? One of the reasons is that the past gives us an identity, because we can 'look back' on what we achieved, on who we think we are.

It confirms and fortifies our usual sense of self. What about the future? Well, the future holds the promise of liberation, and that is also an image we hold in front of our eyes to keep us going, like a carrot in front of a donkey.

The thinking mind has created this whole concept of linear time for practical reasons, but our ego also uses it to convince itself that it is real. As long as our ego keeps relating to it, we are moving backwards and forwards on this imaginary line. We project ourselves into the past and the future, without seeing this precious present moment. When we want to approach this present moment, we see it escapes us again and again. Every sensation we have, is already in the past when it comes into our mind. Finally we recognize that the present moment is out of time. We see that it is impossible – as a person – to 'live in the now' because that person itself is also a concept. As soon as we are in the present moment, we are gone! Then, there is nothing left to say; all there is, is ordinary everyday life appearing in timeless awareness.

In fact, we are incapable of experiencing the duration of a second or a minute, a day or a month. We can think about a minute or a month, we can try to imagine how long that must last, but we will never experience the duration itself. We simply experience what is, and this stream is not to be stopped. In every now-moment, the ungraspable is hidden. Each now-moment is infinite, and as such, inexistent at the same time. When we 'see' this, we come eye to eye with Consciousness. When we look at what happens in this moment, a mystery may appear: this now-moment is essential but at the same time ungraspable. In thirteenth-century China, the poet Wu-men wrote:

A moment is eternity.
Eternity is now.
When you see through that moment,
you see through the one that sees.

That last sentence is very important: when we unmask the present moment, we automatically melt away in what is. During such a moment of clear observation, the personal entity is not relevant at all. When we are alert and awake to the present moment, we are not bothering about the past or the future. We simply melt into the moment, and then that moment is timeless.

8

MELTING AWAY

The pivot of Tao passes through the centre
where all affirmations and denials converge.
He who grasps the pivot is at the still-point
from which all movements and oppositions
can be seen in their right relationship...
Abandoning all thought of imposing a limit
or taking sides,
he rests in direct intuition.

CHUANG TSE

FACE TO SPACE

The whole of life
lies in the verb 'seeing'.

TEILHARD DE CHARDIN

Our models of relationship are based on how people appear to others. When we look at two people who are talking to each other, we see that their faces are in profile: they are face to face with one another, they are distinct and separate. This is true indeed for *other* people: they are face to face with each other. But the inside story is completely different: as a First Person, we do not see our own face. Person D can see the colour of the eyes of person E when they are standing face to face, but we can never see the colour of our own eyes. To further explore the important consequences of this perspective, we are going to do another experiment. It takes two to do this experiment. When we are sitting or standing face to face with our partner, we ask ourselves, 'How many faces are given, on present evidence? We do not *think about it*, we just *see*. When we look at our friend's face, do we also see our own face?... Are we face to face or face to no-face, in our own experience? When we put aside other people's point of view and look for ourselves, how many faces do we then see? Do we see two faces, or one face?... Only one. And what about the near side? Can we see our own face? On the far side we see our friend's face, and on the near side we discover this Transparency we were talking about before.[51]

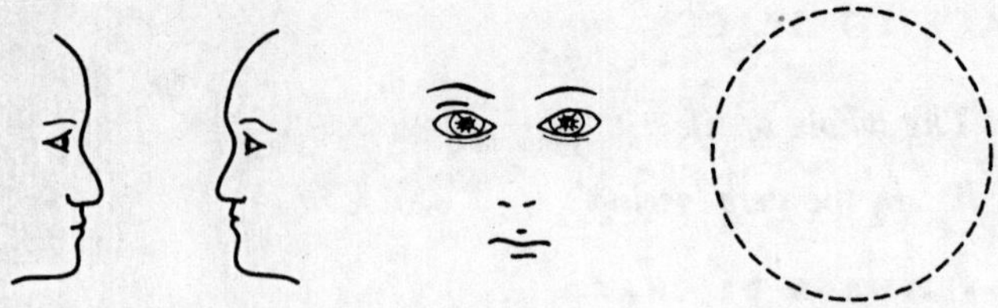

a. outsider's view b. our friend's face c. the Original Face

As we can only see the face of our friend and not our own face, we can conclude that – from this perspective – we do not have a face on our side with which we can keep our friend's face out. On this side, we cannot see eyes. No eyes, no mouth, no face. And this is exactly what Tung Shan discovered while reading the most holy scripture of Mahayana Buddhism, the *Heart Sutra*. The *Heart Sutra* starts off by saying, 'Here, form is void, but the void is also form. Here are no eyes, no nose, no mouth, no ears, no tongue, no functions of those organs'. Douglas Harding says in his workshops: 'Looking at other faces is indeed a great reminder of our own Openness. Face there to no-face here. Face to Space. It doesn't need talking about, just noticing. And as we notice more, it gets easier. It is like undoing an old habit of imagining ourselves behind a face here.' All we have to do is delete the old computer programmes in our head. Why? Because we are used to seeing what we are told to see, what language determines we shall see. We are all conditioned by society that we are a person with a face, we are all programmed (by friends and mirrors) with the idea of having a face here, but in this experiment this belief is put in perspective. All we have to do is take off our sunglasses that colour our perceptions. Then, we can easily recognize our True Nature. The Subject is 'seen' if for a moment we are able to forget the concept about our own face. That is why it is important to forget the drawing with the third person view and really look for ourselves.

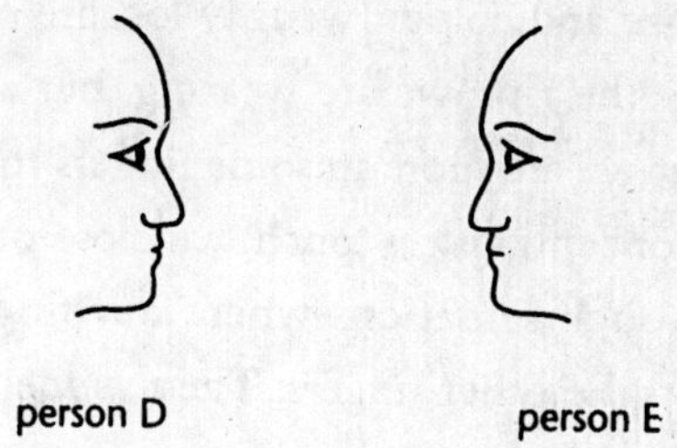

From the outside we (D and E) are of course face to face: a third person (person F, the camera man) can indeed notice that there is a distance between D and E. But only the outsider can see that distance between us. And we (D and E) can only *imagine* that vision by placing ourselves (in imagination) into the head of person F. Indeed, seen from that perspective (third person vision: the point of view of the camera man), we are in confrontation. But from the point of view of the First Person we are open Space, pure and simple.

SEE ME, FEEL ME, TOUCH ME

When in Love,
body, mind, heart and soul
simply do not exist.

RUMI

For the next experiment, we need a partner. It is about discovering Consciousness through one of the other senses: touching. We ask our friend to sit in front of us, and we just hold each other's hands. We can feel the fingers overlapping while we make a tangle of our fingers. When looking at those twenty fingers without moving them, we may indeed notice a difference in size and colour, we may localise our own fingers by recognizing the ring we are wearing, but apart from that, can we say that we are more in some fingers than in others?

Now we concentrate on touch: we close our eyes and just feel the tiny touch sensations where our fingers nudge and slightly overlap the other fingers. Then suddenly – just as we did in the tunnel experiment – we reverse the arrow of our attention so that it points not outward to the sensations of the hands, but inward. We turn our perception around 180 degrees and realize *what is doing the perceiving.* From object (sensation of touch) we go to Subject (the Awareness that allows this perception). This Subject is the white paper we write our story on. It is the unobstructed clearness that accommodates those feelings. It is a kind of pool of awareness in which those sensations float. When we are aware of the four hands as a little nest of warmth, pressure, and touch, we can 'see' (while keeping our eyes closed) that there is no longer a distinction between our hands and the hands of our partner. What we usually take for our separate bodies, now surfaces as one single sensation. It is obvious that we can do this experiment using other body parts than our hands and still 'see' the same oneness. One timeless moment of open attention is enough. And once we have seen it, it is obviousness itself. We will come back to that subject when we talk about Tantra.

There is another important discovery we can make here: we can again 'see' (with the eyes closed!) that there is no longer a distinction between inside and outside. What we notice is that there is no longer a distinction between 'here' (welcoming Awareness) and 'there' (sensation of hands). The latter may need some explanation: it is not that the hands are *out there*, and the perceiving consciousness *in here*. There is only one Space, this clear pool of Awareness, and it contains those four hands together with all other sensations. We can see these sensations unfold within that same awareness. In the beginning, we may indeed imagine that there are two perceptions: one at a distance (the sensations of the four hands), and a second one right here (the awareness). But the second one is not a perception at all. It is the Subject *that contains everything*. So this second one *includes* the first one.

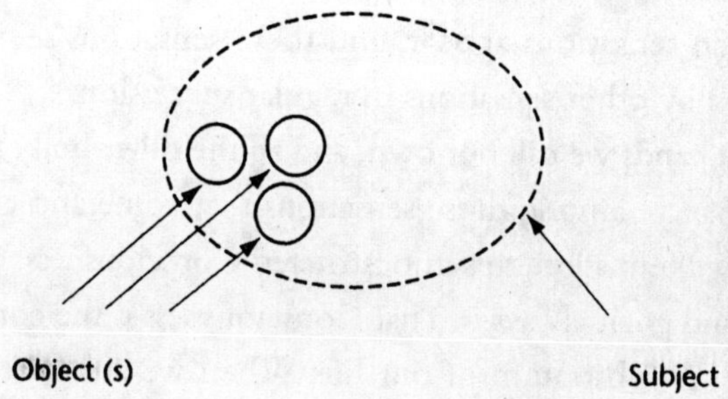

To illustrate the idea of one Subject including all the objects, we use the well-known metaphor of the ocean and the waves. The waves are the phenomena that we witness with our senses (the objects), but their real essence is the ocean (the Subject). The ocean is of course the essence of our being, but we cannot grasp it with our rational mind. How can we ever know what we are? It is impossible. However, when the me-consciousness melts away, the identification with the wave-consciousness disappears and ocean-Consciousness comes to the fore. Then, all is connected with everything else; both the wave and the ocean are essentially water. Then we see that everything in the world is interwoven. It is one universal Energy, and we 'sense' that. This is what the Tibetan Buddhists refer to as 'One Taste'.

This is not seeing with the eyes or feeling with our fingertips. It is rather Consciousness seeing Itself. Our eyes usually look out in search of all kinds of objects or sensations. Our minds are trained to look for sensations but this Seeing is rather the opposite: it is simply the direct witnessing of what we really are. Instead of focussing on objects, we 'see' the Subject. And the latter is what we are. We are aware of capacity, this intensely present emptiness that accommodates all things whatsoever. Sensations inside the body, thoughts and emotions, sensations of our body touching another body, all of these appear in the same Space. We are the transparent consciousness in which sensations appear, and these sensations seem to be replaced by other sensations in regular succession.

The hands we call our own, and all the other body parts we call ours, are among those sensations that come and go. What is taking them all in, this unobstructed Consciousness, does not come and go: it always *is*. That Consciousness is the core of our being, the substratum of our life. When we are aware of the clear Consciousness that is taking in our bodily sensations, that is effortlessly taking in sensations from the so-called environment, we can witness how its emptiness is completely open and available for the pain in our back, for the feeling of hunger or for the sensation of hands touching each other.

Of course, the ocean is only a metaphor for Unity, because the real Ocean can only be observed when we accept duality. We can only observe the waves of the ocean when there is air above the ocean. In that case, there is duality again, there is water and there is air, and there is an observer (e.g. in a plane or on a boat) who is looking at the ocean from above. If the ocean were really the One and All, the observing of this Oneness would be impossible: the observer would be part of the ocean. We would not be a diver, but water itself. While we *are* water it becomes impossible to observe the water, to see the waves, to know the ocean. How can water observe what it is?

NAKED BEINGNESS

> ***Make love to exhaustion, explode.***
> ***Then enter the gap and be aware –***
> ***revelation!***
>
> **VIGYANA BHAIRAVA TANTRA**

Many seekers report that they can lose themselves during meditation. Sometimes it is a very short moment of openness, sometimes it comes to the surface as a major transcendental event. No matter how we feel after the event, such a peak experience can sometimes leave dramatic traces in our minds. There is sometimes a very important shift in consciousness which leads to a very simple but important change in perspective. Such a transcendental event happens when there is a going beyond the concepts of vision X. We put in perspective the concepts we have about ourselves, and are absorbed in a new sense of what we are.

How does this happen? Well, it can not be practiced, it just happens. There seem to be many ways to transcend our senses. Every seeker has got a glimpse of some perfume of the infinite – especially in early childhood – but most people do not seem to remember such glimpses. And since we cannot reach these events with our minds, techniques have been developed to bypass the mind. Especially repetitive actions seem to have the power to act as catalysts in the process of losing ourselves: religious traditions have used a variety of techniques (mantras, prayer, and so on) for that purpose. The danger is of course, that these techniques easily become tools for the ego. In many cases, such transcendental events came spontaneously, without practicing any spiritual techniques. Many people confirm that 'It' happened quite unexpectedly, for example, while walking in a park, waiting for a bus or swimming in a lake. After all, it really does not matter what we are doing, it is all a matter of going *beyond* the senses. Any activity of the body or mind can be a trigger. It is not essential to follow the rules or techniques of one particular spiritual tradition.

In modern western society, many people have lost their 'connection' with prayer or formal meditation. This is partly a result of the association of these spiritual techniques with formal religious organisations. Many seekers – despite their hunger for the spiritual – have turned their backs on official religion. Looking for a more 'natural' way of revealing our infinite nature, some have discovered that we can have a similar shift in consciousness while making love. Without using any exotic techniques, we can discover that an encounter between two people may suddenly open a door to a Space of Beingness – a Space which is clear, simple and as close as can be. Our skin dissolves, our edges melt, and the sense of being 'me' does not reach the surface any more. These are moments when the ego disappears, and we are reduced to air. Then there is no lover, no loved one. We may imagine for example that there is only one body with four arms and four legs, but that is just another image of our mind. The state we are referring to is without concepts: it is bodiless, mindless, timeless. As such it is not a state at all. Ken Wilber wrote:[52]

> For many of the world's great wisdom traditions, particularly in their mature phases, sexuality was deeply viewed as an exquisite expression of spirituality – and a

> path to further spiritual realization. After all, in the ecstatic embrace of sexual love, we are taken beyond ourselves, released from the cramp of the separate self, delivered at least temporarily into timeless, spaceless, blissful union with the wondrous beloved: and what better definition of spiritual release is there than that? We all taste God, taste Goddess, taste pure Spirit in those moments of sexual rapture, and wise men and women have always used that rapture to reveal Spirit's innermost secrets.

Usually people are afraid to lose their body, but in such an intimate encounter they can discover that it can be natural. As we no longer identify with a certain bodily area, or with a special energy that is arising in our subtle body, there is no longer something between the observer and the observed. Instead of an encounter between two people, face to face, there is a completely new approach. Looking at the face of our lover, we could say, 'On the other side I can see a face but on my side there is no face but an open space'. Recognizing this consciously, we have a naked encounter between, on one side, an open space and, on the other side, the sensations of interacting bodies. So, we can discover our true nature by looking in two directions: on one side we see our immediate environment, for instance the face of our friend. At the same time we turn around our arrow of attention in order to discover Who [or What] is seeing. We notice that there are no eyes that are seeing, that there is no brain observing, that there is not even a person who is making love, there is just Consciousness. The one who has experienced this simple but radical change from the thinking ego to the seeing Self may say, 'Even though I still seem to have the habit of feeling bordered by the physical limits of my body, even though I identify all too often with my mental functions like thinking and feeling, I have had a taste of the endless.' Even though we cannot be a hundred percent sure that this is *the* endless, that taste of infinity will never let us go. It has a perfume that reminds us of something indefinable that at the same time is extremely familiar. Intangible like the horizon, always escaping us when we think we are approaching it. Every time we get taken into this Ocean of who we really are, all questions disappear, rationality loses all its importance.

DIVINE INTIMACY

Among the great things
which are to be found among us,
the Being of Nothingness
is the greatest.

LEONARDO DA VINCI

In the games we usually play during the so-called daydream, we see relationships as a confrontation between two people. Many people experience interactions with their partner as an exchange of sensations, feelings and thoughts. It is regarded as an exchange of energy between two separate entities. We can comfort each other with our presence, we can help each other, and we can see the other person as someone who can fulfil a sense of lack in our own life. As long as we limit ourselves to this body-mind machine, there will not be much space left to allow a complete merging with each other: all the space available will be filled with one part meeting another. We all intuitively know that there must be another way to encounter one another.

At a certain moment, there appears a shift in consciousness, similar to moments of pure awareness. Such a timeless moment of transcendence brings our usual way of being into a new perspective. Then, nothing is any longer what it always seemed to be; the thought pattern that makes us think that our partner is a person separate from us breaks down during such a magical moment. During these timeless moments of complete devotion and attention, we may be so wholly absorbed in a specific activity or perception that we lose ourselves. Then, we seem to 'experience' a moment of naked awareness, which is both simple and all-encompassing. Additionally, during such encounters we are no longer in control of the action. The concepts of the ego are melting away, the captain in our head is in a stand-by mode and everything just happens, unpredictably and naturally. Our own personal world, with its expectations and plans, melts away, and we have a taste of the infinite nature of our consciousness. Pattinattar, a Tamil Tantrist said:

> The six spheres of the body, the five states:
> they have all faded away, they have vanished.
> And in the open space I am left with wonderment...
> ungraspable bliss has come over me.

Such an encounter can take us beyond ourselves, to an impersonal Space where our own Centre shines with a glory that time forgot and space cannot imagine. Such a description may sound as if we are referring to something exclusive, but this perspective is universal: discovering this Tantric Space is not affiliated with one particular path, tradition, or religion. It is not exclusively accessible to so-called Tantric masters or magic lovers from the East. This Tantric Space is not some 'state' that has to be 'obtained' or 'achieved' by following specific rules or techniques. There is no entry and no exit. In Zen, this is referred to as the Gateless Gate. When the seeker stands before it, the gate seems to be there. And the seeker hopes to go through the gate one fine day. When it is clear that there is nobody inside, all these concepts collapse. As soon as it is seen that there is no seeker, the gate disappears. No one ever passes through it, nobody will ever look back, simply because there was never anybody there in the first place. Losing our concepts about ourselves, all that is left is 'what is', without any further comments or plans.[53]

When we move beyond our thinking, we lose our usual sense of separation, and we may be overwhelmed by the most powerful sense of 'I'. What a wonderful discovery it is to be with our lover and to be able to discover a sense of identity that we never imagined before. On the one hand we seem to disappear completely, and on the other hand it is as if we are filled with an endless Space of Love. So there is a sense of fullness and emptiness at the same time.

All we see is the 'Is-ness' in everything; it is seen in the partner, it is seen in ourselves, it is seen in the encounter, it is seen in the environment. In fact, there are no separate entities any more; it is so simple and so obvious that it is almost embarrassing to put this on paper. What seems to happen is that we vanish into thin air: we are out of the world and yet fully present. And we can check it out right now. When we focus on 'I Am' with our eyes closed, we discover that this 'I Am' has no location. Out of a habit, we think that 'I Am' is confined to the body, but if we watch carefully we realize that the sense 'I Am' is not limited in any way. This Space has no residence in our heart or brain or anywhere else.

THE ART OF CONSCIOUS SEX

We dissolve –
smiling, moaning, weeping –
in the openhearted bliss of sexual embrace.[54]

DAVID DEIDA

When the separation between the body and its immediate environment is abolished in a so-called Tantric encounter, we stop pretending to be something or someone we are not. We lose the identification with our body-mind machine, we stop expecting and we let everything be *as it is*. There is only an effortless allowing, be it of perceptions of sounds, sexual sensations, thoughts or feelings passing by. Everything is equally allowed to come into existence, not as a practice, but because it cannot be any other way. If we become aware of our Consciousness, we find ourselves wide awake. When we simply live in welcoming the spaceless here and the timeless now, we have a foretaste of what the lost paradise might have felt like.

As soon as we have tasted this paradise, we want it again. As soon as we had a glimpse of it, we want more of it. And that is when the trouble begins. We organise life (living in a certain way, becoming vegetarian, doing meditation, practising Eastern love techniques) in order to *get it again*. But that is not the way these things work. As long as there is technique (yoga technique, Tantra technique, meditation technique), there must be a doer of the technique, there must be an achiever of experiences. As long as there is control (control of breath, control of energy, control of orgasm, control of mind), there must be a controller. This means that there remains a state of dualism. As long as we cling to what we are supposed to feel, as long as we hope to experience what we have read in the popular textbooks about Tantra and Taoism, we continue to identify ourselves with our personality. The more we try to imitate the so-called experts, no matter if we think we succeed or not, the more we reinforce our bondage to the ego. Nothing is wrong with all these paths and techniques, as long as we realize that they are no more than (pleasurable) side tracks.

When we completely let go the craving for the transcendental, we may see all this in a new perspective. Leaving behind any form of control or suppression, we surrender to what nature has to offer us. It may offer us peaks and valleys, it does not matter how long we are riding the waves: it is happening out of time anyway. There is no doer, no experiencer, no partner, just being, just a meeting in the emptiness. Such a 'meeting' can be described as a naked encounter between lovers. It is an experience of being together without imposing any demands. In the spaceless and the timeless there is no room for possessiveness or future perspective; there is only space for being together, there is just room for friendship without reservations. And even that is an exaggeration; there is only that which happens and in that happening, a magic Space can appear in which we lose ourselves and find the other. In that Tantric Space our friend then has the opportunity to express himself or herself entirely. The partner can be himself or herself and does not have to fulfil specific conditions to receive our attention, love or approval. This can be very liberating for both partners.

THE GATE TO YOUR LOVE

If you wish to be free,
know you are the Self,
the witness of all these,
the heart of awareness.

ASHTAVAKRA GITA

We said that when there is no doer, no experiencer, we just seem to disappear for our lover. Then, there is no meeting between two people, just a meeting in the emptiness. But there is no need for a particular sexual technique: this Open Space is equally accessible in silence, without moving, without sexual intercourse. In such encounters we literally give ourselves away, while at the same time we are not 'doing' anything. We completely let go the most valuable thing we think to possess: our sense of self-identity, our personality in which we have invested throughout our entire life. In a timeless moment we lose our existence as a person.

This demands an ability to detach from ourselves, to detach from our identification patterns and from our conditionings. Everything happens then naturally: an unknowable process takes place automatically. This process is as if we are carried away by the stream of sexual energy: the 'me' disappears and what remains is the encounter with the partner. When we disappear for our lover, we 'see' something which totally transforms our whole perception of life. Something that is greater and more wonderful than anything we can imagine, and when this shift is appearing, it is happening within the timelessness of what is.

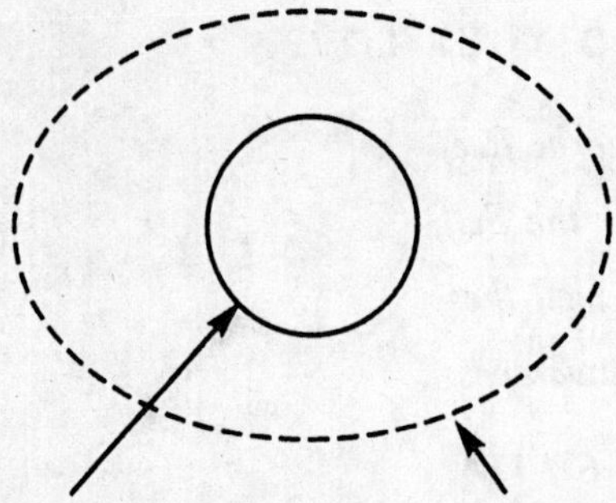

As pointed out earlier on, all this has nothing to do with acrobatic or secret sex techniques. What we are talking about here is the simple and the breathtaking magnificence of the *ordinary*. Immediately here is the seeing of what we are. What just happened to us – we can only reflect on it afterwards – is unique and transient, and simple and wonderful. All we have to 'do' is *be aware of what is* – does that sound difficult? Simply melting away. All of a sudden we discover [it is discovered] that we are actually the one and only Origin of all there is. When there is a letting go even of the one who is aware, all that remains is Presence itself. Life just lives itself through us and we are the Witness of it, lost in Presence, observing it all in that same space-less here and timeless now. When such Presence is 'seen', any notion of space or time is gone, and Witness and Presence become one.

To illustrate this, we can use the following metaphor: we make three drawings in the sand on the sandy beach with our finger: one drawing of a square, one of a triangle and one of a circle. These three images correspond to three different states: the first one of two people who are together but who face each other as separate beings, the second one of two people who live a moment of bliss, and the third one of two people disappearing for each other. The last one may be referred to as a Tantric encounter of two beings absorbed in the flow of their meeting.

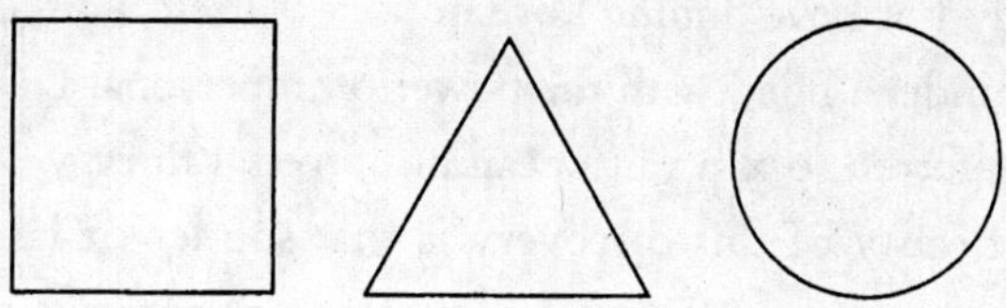

a. square b. triangle c. circle

These three 'states' are not the only possibilities: as long as our attention is focussed on the three drawings, we do not see the sand around and in between the three drawings. When we take a closer look, we notice the sand around and between the drawings, which, in this analogy is the common background of these three states, and in fact the common space for *all* sensations. Having seen this background does not prevent us from still seeing the three drawings, and yet seeing It makes all the difference. Recognizing this silent Space does not prevent us from noticing the differences between these three states and enjoying each state for what it is. This 'broader' vision still allows us to notice their specific characteristics, but we 'see' that there is only unity connecting all: there is only sand.

Many people say that it is wonderful to be able to share this vision with a friend. They sense the immense openness of impersonal Love that can appear in such a meeting. In this core of our fundamental nature, there is a seed of infinity perceived in the very centre of our Self, and from this seed the infinite nurtures our life. Then we know ourselves in the immediacy of the moment. All our spiritual longings are suddenly gone now. This is sometimes referred to as a felicity without cause, a happiness that is not dependent on external objects or situations, a deep joy that is different from any other object-generated happiness. This is not a surrender to a love 'of' something or somebody, but Love finding Love in Itself as Itself. This 'Tantric Space' is indeed filled with the power of impersonal Love, and may be referred to as a vast ocean of universal Energy.

The beauty of this discovery is that sooner or later this Clarity takes over our heart in such depth of compassion that our personal expectations and goals seem to drop away. Unconditional love comes to the surface spontaneously without our personal interference, and we finally understand the core message of Buddhism (and of any spiritual tradition), which is true compassion for all that is. True compassion for our fellow people simply is there, without the urge to try and change people, without the desire to be a good person: just unconditional compassion. The only danger with these words is that we personalize this 'unconditional compassion' and think that we have to *feel* this in some way or another. Then, we are again in the wheel of waiting for experiences of divine love, which is again a subtle game of the seeking mind.

9

AWARENESS WAKES UP

This 'awakening' into Awareness,
this view of Reality,
Is no place at which you can arrive,
no accomplishment which you can achieve,
no goal which you can attain.
It is your Original Nature,
which you simply Recognize
in a profound and stunning moment
of rediscovery.[55]

METTA ZETTY

BEING OR KNOWING?

The Self, though One,
takes the shape of every object
in which It dwells

THE UPANISHADS

Some mystics say that true Freedom or complete Liberation is only possible when the personality is not claiming the central role. If that is true, what can we do to 'get' Liberation? Where can we go? Our personality always wants to have a goal. Our mind always wants to focus on something new. Or on something personal. But how can the personality do something when it is supposed not to be there? Are we getting out of our minds? How can the personal mind discover the *Impersonal*? Isn't the mind checkmated now? Instead of associating with what comes and goes, with thoughts and concepts, it is sometimes suggested that we (who?) can also *stay with Awareness itself*. The joke is that we do not have to do anything for it. What could we do in order to be what we already are, anyway? The same mystics also say that although we 'are already It', we just have to *recognize* It. So, there is a difference. We have to realize It, we have to recognize what we already are, our True Nature. And they say that our true nature is the clear sky and not the clouds. In the beginning, it is easier to recognize our true nature in moments of silence (and not in the noise of our thoughts and feelings). They even suggest that we have the *choice* to put our attention on the Silence or to put our attention on the noise. They say that it is just a matter of letting our attention being filled with the blue sky instead of the clouds. In this metaphor, the clouds stand for our personal thoughts, ambitions, hopes and fears. These clouds are said to prevent us from seeing the sunshine. And the clear sky stands for the quiet and clear background which is witnessing all these images. Our mind always has the habit to look for new sensations. The clouds seem to be more attractive to the mind than the empty sky. That is part of its design. Ideas come and go, sensations in the body come and go, emotions come and go, just like in a movie. What about the background in which they appear? What if we no longer choose to 'feed' the mind with new thoughts and concepts? Concepts and sensations come and go, but where is That which never comes and goes? What if we focus our attention on That? What about *being* this Source without thinking about it? What about being this Background without trying to understand it? This is beyond the beyond. If we disappeared in this Vastness, if we melted into the Clarity that we are, the thinking mind would become unemployed. The mind would be left with nothing to hold on to.

Usually, through identification with our mind, our thoughts become compulsive. This is true for many seekers. The thoughts that come up – we are not talking here about practical thoughts, but about egocentric thoughts, thoughts about our personal past and future – cannot be stopped and seem to be leading their own life. Since most people are not able to stop this thinking process, they are overruled by their thought patterns and they don't even realize that. The usual *identification* with the train of thoughts (the so-called thinking mind) is only energizing this process. Giving thoughts a lot of attention adds even more power to the thought process and creates a smoke-screen of labels. We cover our own world with a veil of judgements, and it is said that this incessant mental noise prevents people from finding the silence and the clarity of Naked Being. This inner voice comments, speculates and complains. As a result, people do not see clearly because they perceive and judge the present through the eyes of the past, or the future. In other words, they live in a conceptual world. When our senses are used without interference, we look without interpreting. We see light, shapes and colours without judging them. We are aware of the silent presence of every object we perceive. We are aware of the Space that allows all sensations to be, and in fact nothing changes. It is not a different perception we are referring to here, nothing 'new' or 'different' is discovered, it is just a question of a new perspective. When we are not involved in thinking about the past or the future, there is an ease and lightness in what is being done. There is no resistance to what is, there is no complaining, because all our attention is absorbed in whatever the present moment presents.

LIKE BUBBLES IN SPARKLING WATER

> *What is troubling us is the tendency*
> *to believe that the mind*
> *is like a little man within.*
>
> **LUDWIG WITTGENSTEIN**

How can we see our true nature? How can we wake up from the daydream? How can our (limited) mind know the (infinite) awareness? Will this book give the final answers? No. We will not know and neither have we ever known. All we can do is – at a certain point – give up searching, letting go all our longing and striving. We (who?) give up 'wanting to know'. Once there is a dedication to what is, then this 'openness' becomes a continuous and living meditation, and thereafter there seems to be no reason why one should formalise it into a technique (meditation, prayer, devotion) that is separated from everyday life. It is happening in this room while reading this book, right now. Thinking that spiritual techniques and following the rules of one specific religious tradition is going to bring us closer to 'realization' is just another belief system. Similarly, reincarnation and karma are concepts of vision X, which encourage the idea of a separate self who thinks to have free choice to do right or wrong and be rewarded or punished in future lives. As we said before, all of these concepts are not relevant if we are looking for our true nature.

Everything that we witness in our life is totally unique and fresh and innocent. It comes and goes, it is here and then it is gone. When – as a little experiment – we ask ourselves where our thoughts come from, we can notice that they are not ours. We close our eyes for one minute, and just try to 'catch' a thought as soon as it comes up. We try to 'catch' our thoughts as soon as possible, if we can. Where do these thoughts come from? Are they really 'our' thoughts? Are we 'producing' them ourselves, or are they just appearing in our awareness, like clouds that appear in the sky? When we look carefully, we witness that they emerge, seemingly from nowhere, and rise up, have their moment and then recede to nothing. In other words, thoughts and emotions originate from nowhere, just like bubbles appear from seemingly nowhere in a glass of sparkling water. They come from no particular source, rise up to the surface, and then disappear. They come from infinity and go back to infinity.[56]

The infinite is all there is, and as a consequence the rules or standards that our minds would set up for any kind of spiritual awakening simply do not apply. There is no one to prepare for liberation, as there is no one to be liberated. There are no rules because there is no real path. No conditions are required prior to awakening. We are talking here about an awakening – not as an event or a state of mind – but as an energy, and even that word can become misleading. It is simply *universal Energy*, in the sense that it is the source of all. This energy is all-encompassing, neutral and impersonal.

We can see a plane flying in the sky, but when asked 'What do you see?' people say, 'A plane'. The blue sky itself is overlooked. A plane comes and goes, the sky is always there. This sky – which contains the plane – is what we want to refer to. And it is clear that referring to the Sky is not about getting anything or going anywhere. To 'have' or to 'get' something is only possible if there is both a 'someone' and a 'something' to get, which is not the case in this quest for our true Identity. This book is not about a spiritual quest in the usual sense of the word. There is no 'searcher' and there is no 'goal' because finally we understand that there is nothing to get. Of course, the body and our thoughts and feelings appear to be very personal, and so does the spiritual quest, but that is only a trick of the mind. That is how our senses are designed and nothing is wrong with it. In fact, all those passing sensations may indeed appear to be personal but they have nothing to do with our First Person. As soon as we see that we do not need this imaginary personality in order to find Liberation, we can just drop it and allow our life to happen without there being any illusory central captain. But the ego is equipped with a mind that goes on and on asking questions, judging everything. When we (who?) give up the captain, we are afraid that then we will live in chaos because we give up control and security. We realize that we will be left hopeless and helpless.[57] But what really happens is that we can finally fall in love with our life as it is presenting itself: we accept what is, right here, right now, without knowing what is going to happen next. What a relief to just 'let go' and live without this inner voice judging everything we think or do. Tony Parsons says: 'So relax and let it all happen – because it will anyway. The relief is letting go of this apparent inner voice which is telling you how you should act or be. Just drop it now, right here'. While reading this, we may get a sense of something that watches these thoughts arising and receding. It feels as though there is 'something above and behind' that is watching right now. A kind of Witness that is not capable of judging, only *simply seeing*. It is not our inner voice that is talking to us, it is not some higher energy form, it is a kind of blank Space that is totally without concern for what is happening. And it is not above us, not outside us, because it is everywhere. Seeing this Space has nothing to do with making our minds still and killing our egos. Being able to recognize *This* has nothing to do with purification or behaving in a specific way. It is about recognizing what we *are*, and what we are is the still, silent awareness that sees the mind and its activities. So, what we are is just *behind* what we perceive (and also *in* what we perceive). This Presence just sits there and waits for us to unmask our daydream and see the traffic of our minds. Once that becomes clear, we have a completely different 'taste' about what we are. Then, reading this book becomes obsolete.

WHO DIES?

There is only Light.
There is only Being.[58]

TONY PARSONS

When we identify with the ego, with our so-called third person (vision X), we all have to live with that most inescapable of certainties: the common-sense fact that you and I are lined up in death row awaiting execution. There is no question of whether we die, but only a question of when we will die. However inevitable our own death may be, the crucial question is if death is really the end? Can we accept the fact that the light will just be turned off? If we are made of perishable stuff, there is no other solution: once we are dead, the game is over. Once the heart stops beating, the brain will run out of oxygen and quite soon after that, *the movie is over.* Still we feel that this cannot be true. Our body may be made of perishable stuff, but what about our spirit or soul? Our personality finds it hard to accept the fact of disappearing, and therefore invents an afterlife or reincarnation. Most people believe in a soul (or some form of subtle energy) that transcends the body and that lives on after the death of this body. Western religions suggest that this soul is going somewhere (hell, heaven) after we die, but that is all based on belief systems. It is interesting to see that the mind will try to find any way in which it can continue after death. The mind will create several scenarios – appealing or threatening – for the idea to continue in some form or another. People seem to be afraid of disappearing for ever, and their minds just make up the rest. Religious organisations are of course stimulating these ideas of vision X: they do so by creating concepts like holy and evil, and stories about heaven and hell. In a similar way, Eastern religions have their own belief systems: reincarnation and karma are also concepts of vision X and also encourage the idea of a separate self who can choose between right or wrong and who will be punished or rewarded for his choices.

Most seekers do not realize that one of the main characteristics of the future is that it will always be in the future. So, why should we waste our time in thinking about the future? Why worry about our death? Why do we want to know what will happen when we die, before we know what we are *now*? Again, the solution of our problem with our future lies in our present. We can discover right now that we are not incarnate anyway. If we do not believe it, we can have it confirmed by our own direct experience, by doing that little experiment where we close our eyes for a minute and take the time to find where our personality (our so-called third person) lives. We try to find an ego inside our body or mind. Can we find it? Where is it located exactly? Let us really try and find it, right now! Where is it?... We have to admit that we will not be able to find such a person inside; we just know it as a concept. We discovered this before: nobody is Home! What about our First Person? Can we find where that One is living? Our true Essence is not to be found because it is invisible. And it does not live inside our brain; it never was in this perishable body, although sensations of our perishable body appear in 'It' on a regular basis. The First Person is the Consciousness in which all these images and concepts appear. It has been hidden *everywhere*, and that is why we don't see It.

We have asked this question before: are we really locked up in the prison of our body (vision X), or are we awareness which is free and unbounded (vision Y)? When we look down at our body, at that trunk, those legs and arms, and we witness what we see, are we really locked up in there? [Please, check it out!] Or are we just witnessing parts of this body? With the latter in mind, we could say that we are already free and wide-ranging! Although we seem limited to our body when we rely on our sensory perceptions, there is another 'level' which goes beyond the limitation of our senses and our mind. On the physical level, however, we are indeed limited to our body. There is no doubt about that. We cannot feel the pain of the person sitting next to us, nor can we feel his or her emotions. That is how the human senses work, that is the way our body-mind machine is designed, and there is nothing wrong with that. On that level, we do indeed seem to be separate: that is the game of vision X. The game of the third person. The game of the sandcastle that knows that his or her castle is perishable. Dust to dust, sand to sand. But when it is discovered – for example during one of the awareness experiments or during a sudden transcendental event – that what we really are is Consciousness, there is a completely new perspective regarding death. Now we may understand that the sand which was there before our castle was born, will not disappear after we die. Our True Nature is here before, during and after the manifestation of our life. Then, it is clear that 'our' sand grains will still be there when 'our' castle dies. The castle will not have its original shape any more, but not one grain of sand can escape. Of course, what we really are is both, because both the castle and the beach are made of grains of sand. As long as we live, we appear to be a sandcastle (vision X): that is what our senses tell us. But at the same time we can 'see' that we are made of grains of sand (vision Y), and as such we are not limited to this particular body and mind. The first one (vision X) tells us we are temporary and personal, the second one (vision Y) makes it clear we are timeless and impersonal, and cannot die.[59]

BEYOND LIFE AND DEATH

There is just a flash of insight
without anyone being there
who thinks he or she has understood it.

RAMESH BALSEKAR

It is worth noting that so-called Seers generally have taught that finding our True Nature includes the discovery that we are neither the body nor are we in the body, but that the body is in 'Us'. Discovering this for ourselves – not just reading about it – may feel as if we are extending to the farthest reaches of the cosmos, that our Consciousness is the one and same consciousness that is enveloping all minds and all persons. Now we understand when such Seers say that our True Nature goes beyond personal aspirations, beyond death. Of course, our psychophysical ego says that it has a history and a future; it pretends that it goes through a process, a development, and we have to admit that indeed the story seems to be very real. But that is exactly the magic of the daydream. It looks so real and as a result everybody is hypnotised by it.

However, the so-called 'Final Perceiver' remains outside such temporal processes: Awareness does not, at our death, vanish from our view, it is we who vanish from Its view. When we rest in observing Awareness – watching the concepts about body and mind float by – we might begin to notice that what we are actually feeling is simply a sense of freedom, a sense of release, a sense of not being bound to any of the mental images we are witnessing. When we simply rest in this vast openness, we see that the Final Witness is not out there in the stream; it is the vast openness in which the (apparent) stream arises. It was never born, It will never die. And because It is Unborn, It is Undying. Chuang-tzu said:

> All that has form, sound, colour,
> may be classed under the head of thing.
> But one can attain to formlessness
> and vanquish death.

Consciousness was not created with our body, it will not perish when our body perishes. It is not that it lives on beyond our body's death, but rather that it never enters the wheel of life and death in the first place. It does not live on after our body, it lives *prior* to our body. It does not go on in time forever, but is out of time altogether. It is simply beyond all concepts of space, time and logical thought.

The mind of the separate ego wants perpetuity of the personality through a theory of an afterlife. The mind cannot accept that the personality will be like a bubble on the surface of the water, disappearing some day into the Beingness of infinity that it has always been. Of course, nobody knows how it feels when we die, what exactly happens when we fall back into this Beingness. But on the other hand, being familiar with the Transparency we have been referring to before, it may be possible that seeing the Transparency right now is exactly the same as the Transparency that awaits us when we die. Douglas Harding says:[60]

> What you look like is perishable. I am in receipt of what you look like, and I regret to have to say that it is perishing. I look round, and I cannot see any permanence in this room. If I go outside and look at the stars, even they are perishing. Galaxies are perishing, let alone the planet, let alone mountains, let alone nations and cities. Every thing perishes. But there is one thing that doesn't perish, and that is the Reality from which the appearances are coming. What's at the centre of my life and of your life is not perishing because there is nothing to perish. There is only Awareness at the center, and Awareness is not biodegradable. It doesn't perish.

Democratic spirituality

You are like a mirage in the desert,
which the thirsty man thinks is water;
but when he comes up to it
he finds it is... nothing.

AL-ALAWI

We all want to believe that we are Infinity, but there is no need to *believe* this. This vastness that we are is quite full and obvious by Itself. We just have to release our notions of, 'Then I had it for a second, but now I lost it', or 'One day, I will become enlightened', or 'One day, I may be experiencing this infinity all the time'. Let us make this clear right away. There will never be a day that we can say, 'I have found my infinite nature'. It is a contradiction in terms. Although some spiritual teachers have a tendency to *personalize* their so-called spiritual experiences, we should not pay attention to them. It easily creates a distance and separation between teacher and devotees. That is not the way this game is played. We have to remember that this book is about what is the *same* in you and me and everybody else, not what seems to be different. Anyway, if we do believe such teachers, they have really taken us for a ride – no matter how holy or sincere they may appear to be. Nobody can ever experience pure Awareness. We simply have to remember that we will never be able to say, 'I am walking around in an awakened state'. Although this Infinity is boundless in all directions, we will never experience It because it is what we are. It is what *everybody* is. That is why we call the approach in this book democratic spirituality: we do not accept any form of hierarchy.

Recognizing this leaves us in wonder with no reference to anyone having an experience. This Consciousness is what we all are. We just noticed it, while others do not seem to notice it. So, we just recognized it, that's all. Then there may be the natural notion of Being without limits. And that does bring us back to the very basic issues of this book. The open secret is *everywhere*, it is not hidden in the sacred scriptures, it is not exclusive for those who are in a special state of mind. There is no need to look for *This* in the religious or the ecstatic. It is in plain everyday life and we do not have to become spiritual in any sense to rediscover the Source of life. We can 'see' the Infinite everywhere. This is about the recognition of the Infinite in the common things. We just forget about the spiritual and the mystic. There is no need for holy books to see This. As Tony Parsons says, 'It is as much in you or me as it is in the carpet or in the sound of a car passing by in the street'. This revaluing of the 'simplicity and ordinariness' of Awakening is of course nothing new. For example, it is one of the highlights of Zen. For Zen Buddhists, even the making of a cup of tea is like a 'holy ritual'. No need for sculptures of Gods and Saints, no need for religious ceremonies or burning incense. How could we ever symbolize It in a particular way when It is everywhere? Only the abstract can come close here. The Seeing we are referring to in this book goes beyond intellectual understanding and beyond belief or religion. We cross the borders of the intellectual and devotional, where words and symbols – even the most sacred ones – simply fail to express what we are trying to refer to. Any form of religious representation becomes obsolete, because 'This' cannot be imagined. As a result, all the spiritual symbolic representations are misleading. All those magic formulas, all those holy books do not suffice here. Not one representation of 'It' can come close to 'It' because this Space is beyond any symbol or concept. Even art directly referring to the mystic or religious is too specific. Maybe the abstract in contemporary art can come close in some cases.[61] For example, American 'colorfield painters' like Mark Rothko and Barnett Newman attempted to evoke the infinite in their large chromatic abstractions.[62] When the spectator learns to discount the surface of the painting, so that the whole painting ceases to *be* as a separate object, its mystical or spiritual character, its transcendental beauty, may become evident. As such, it can become a *pointer* to the Infinite. Still, we must realize that any attempt to represent 'It' is doomed to fail. The frame of an abstract painting is as much an expression of the Infinite as the painting itself.

What is left then? Well, there is only Oneness, and maybe the natural notion of being without limits. Simply being with what is, without anyone claiming It, without anyone trying to turn it into a religious system with symbols, rules, expectations and spiritual heroes. So, this coming Home to our True Self is not exclusive for the saints we see represented in the churches and temples, it is for you and me. Nobody is excluded from It because we *are* It. It is so ordinary, so obvious, so natural. We just fail to pay full attention to It, but most of us cannot believe that It can be as simple and obvious as that. And as a result, we do not realize that *this is It*. Everybody has the potential of living in this vastness, we all 'have' an awakened nature but we are not paying attention to It. Some teachers say that when we (who?) are paying more attention to this ease of being – for example through a simple switch of perception – we are allowing our attention to rest in this infinite emptiness. In this emptiness there is at the same time a wholeness: everything is infinite, completely as it is. This infinite Space is not some kind of spiritual utopia or paradise, it is the most common place on earth: indeed, we can recognize this Infinity both in the sunset over the ocean as in pain, failure and ugliness. Nothing is excluded.

10

FROM ILLUSIONS TO CLARITY

The nature of liberation is direct, simple and as

natural as breathing.

Many will come across it and shuffle quickly

back

to that which they think they know and do.

But there are those with whom the invitation

will resonate…

they will suddenly see and be ready to let go of

all seeking,

even for that which they have called

enlightenment.[63]

TONY PARSONS

NOWHERE TO GO

Out there, behind the thoughts
of doing good and doing bad, is a Field.
There I am waiting for you.

RUMI

In meditation there are moments when no one seems to be there any more, that there is simply a vast open nothingness which also feels very peaceful and alive. Such testimonies of transcendental events are reported in all spiritual traditions, but when the seekers cease the meditation and then 'come back' to their everyday life, that space of inner peace is not apparent any more. They conclude that they have 'found' it, but at the same time they are frustrated because they seem to 'have lost it' when the bliss is over. This inner fight will continue as long as the seeker does not see that the Infinite is available everywhere, even when not being meditative.[64]

This undivided Presence is available in any situation and when it is first recognized it may indeed seem to be very intense, blissful or peaceful: there is an initial recognition which is sometimes very spectacular. The good side of such an event is that the seeker gets a direct recognition of 'what is'. Such a 'seeing' may blow away many conditionings, and that cannot be found through reading a book. But the danger is that the seeker personalizes this event, and says, 'On the first of April, I have experienced the infinite', or 'I have found my divine nature and now I am a spiritual teacher'. The seeker imagines he or she has become a 'finder' and does not realize that he or she is back in a personal game. He believes his inner voice which says, 'I have found Infinity, but the others are still looking for It'.

When we understand that our inherent nature is not limited to our personal life but that it is all-encompassing, we discover a Beingness that is not dependent on particular circumstances or a special state of mind. When we see that what we are is clear Awareness, we rediscover a Presence that does not depend on our personal circumstances. This is not a fulfilment that depends on our feelings or thoughts, it is just 'what is'. Nathan Gill says:[65]

> When you no longer seriously entertain the whole conceptual story of a life extended in thought beyond the present content of awareness, conceptual living is seen for what it is and ceases to be the exclusive focus of attention.

When we realize that all we 'need' is with us right now and that we can access It fully without becoming special or spiritual in any way, we can call off the spiritual search. None of the striving, chasing and looking outside of ourselves is going to provide the 'seeker in us' true fulfilment or complete liberation. 'It' is not a reward that will be given us at the end of the trip. We are all craving unconditional love, we all have the certainty that we deserve that connectedness with the infinite. We all seem to miss our Original State, and those among us who had a glimpse of 'It' desperately want it back in some way or another. The problem is that we may easily start to look in the wrong direction. As we said repeatedly, most people are looking for a higher energy, want to copy a spiritual hero, hope to 'get' a special divine state that goes with paranormal skills, in order to find spiritual liberation. And a lot of seekers are convinced that they have to be purified in order to become worthy for This. All these belief systems confirm our personalities that look for (personal) spiritual growth and they imitate the so-called great masters who said they have found It themselves through grace or through decades of discipline. Other teachers believe that they have 'received' It from their own master and suggest their own followers hope for the same process of transmitting the flame. And the disciples believe that they have a good chance of reaching that same spiritual level as the master, if only they stay in his neighbourhood, give all their devotion to the master, behave the same way as their teacher does or at least do what their spiritual hero asks them to do (changing their diet, accepting a new name, living according to the rules of that particular spiritual organization, and so on). And as these seekers are all desperately looking for that taste of oneness, they are easily misled. They do not realize that the spiritual game is personalized. They had a transcendental event, and from then on they are very vulnerable because they want that feeling of peace and oneness again, and secretly they hope that they will be in bliss for ever by following the rules of that religious system. In other words, they want to climb the mountain of spirituality until they reach the top. They believe their master is already at the top, but do not realize that Consciousness has no hierarchy. The infinite does not see anyone as 'higher' than anyone else. Consciousness does not value a moment of bliss as higher than a moment of pain. If everything is One Energy, how could it matter?

As a result, it is useless to follow the rules of a spiritual school, and misleading to try and imitate spiritual heroes. Our search for spiritual authority is in fact an avoidance of the inherent challenge of everyday living itself.[66] Why do we need a guru or teacher to live our lives, when we realize that there is nothing to 'get'? How can somebody *else* show us what *we* are? Gurus and teachers can only tell us what *we are not*, and as such they can be important catalysts in discovering what we are not. But nobody can tell us what we really are. No matter what the spiritual authorities claim to be for themselves, no matter what their followers are suggesting, no matter how important some teachers may be, it is all very misleading if we take the spiritual quest personally. Then, all of it easily becomes a mind game. Eastern mystical literature has stimulated so-called spiritual seekers to expect ecstatic peak experiences for themselves. This is a result of these books being full of stories of special people (avatars, bodhisattvas) who are said to be in a continuous higher state. Maybe some gurus really are in some kind of exotic higher state, but does it really matter? Is this quest about examining other people's states? What is the point of comparing? Where are the boundaries? Who is separated from whom? And if Consciousness is One, where are the so-called others? As Nathan Gill[67] says, 'If all is Consciousness, why are you still seeking?' In the end, nothing is wrong with all these spiritual paths creating expectations and frustrations among the seekers. We do not want to judge all these spiritual belief systems, we even do not judge the teachers misleading their followers. It is just the game of spiritual seeking.

This book does not focus on imitating a specific mystic tradition or spiritual path. The reflections in this book are designed to invite us to discover another possibility which is simple, direct and independent from any religion or teacher. Although we have found a lot of inspiration in all these spiritual teachers and mystical traditions, we realize that there is nobody to become enlightened, no person to be liberated. That all this imitating and comparing is useless. Once that is realized, all the above dilemmas disappear immediately.

THERE ARE NO RULES

Awareness simply is and you are That.
It has nothing to do with great sacrifice or intelligence.
You are already That.[68]

TONY PARSONS

When we approach the issue of discovering the infinite Consciousness in our daily lives, we think we can learn to live how to be this Pure Consciousness. But is trying to accomplish that not as ridiculous as asking how rain learns to rain? How does the sun learn to shine? What has water to do in order to become wet? As we pointed out before, we are already whatever it is that we are seeking. When our basic nature is Pure Consciousness, this means that we are infinite, omnipresent and impersonal. As such, there is nothing that we have to do, nothing in particular we have to get rid of, nothing spiritual to meditate on. As long as we believe in the personality, we believe we can somehow 'change' this personality into something better. Trying to make ourselves more relaxed or more spiritual by using specific meditation techniques may look interesting at a superficial level [and at that level nothing is wrong with it!] but it has absolutely no value when Liberation is concerned. As we said earlier, all spiritual techniques – no matter how subtle they are – can become tools for the ego, and can only be effective on that level. They can leave us with a peaceful ego, and so what? It is like a woman standing in front of a mirror and trying to look more attractive by putting make-up *on the mirror glass.* In other words, it is all meaningless. Understanding that leaves us with nothing to do, nowhere to go. And some authors say that if we dare to give up our concepts about our spiritual quest unconditionally, all that is left is Openness, and the understanding that there is no reason to become different from what we are right now. Justus Kramer Schippers says:[69] 'It is as it is, it cannot be any other way, and it is enough to realize that.'

When we really see that every spiritual effort comes from the ego, we understand why some teachers dare to confirm the meaninglessness of spiritual techniques. With the above mentioned reflections in mind, the uselessness of any spiritual path is clear now. All these holy scriptures, all these sacred scriptures, all these religious rules, now we see that it only has value when it comes to satisfying the spiritual ambitions of the ego. Really understanding this may leave us confused and helpless, but it is also a door to complete freedom. There are no rules any more, and in that way the meaninglessness of religious traditions is not a real problem at all.

So, as we said before, all the efforts we make to come closer to Liberation are like putting make-up on the mirror face. Maybe we will finally get a nice reflection in the mirror, but what is the point? Does that change our Original Face? Is getting a nicer ego what the quest in this book is all about? Is this the path that will bring us to eternity? Meister Eckhart, the German Christian mystic (1260–1328) said:

> For whoever seeks God in some special Way, will gain the Way and lose God who is hidden in the Way. But whoever seeks God without any special way, finds Him as He really is... and He is life itself.

When we realize this, does it mean that we have to throw away all the spiritual practices, that all these therapies and books are wrong? Does this imply that we just have to forget about yoga and meditation? That all religious systems are sidetracks? There is no answer to this question, because there is no right or wrong anyway, and both religion and meditation may be appropriate, just as everything else is appropriate. So, nothing is obligatory, nothing is forbidden. There are simply no rules. Even when we say that some people may need meditation or spiritual exercises in order to become – one day – more 'open' to Naked Awareness, what is the value of such a statement when we realize that time is an illusion. And – as a result – this *future* Liberation is also an illusion?

The Abandonment of Seeking

In allowing presence, however,
we embrace a kind of death.
What dies is all expectation,
judgement and effort to become.[70]

TONY PARSONS

As long as we live, our body is still apparent and the 'seeing' happens in relation to that body-mind. But that does not mean that this seeing depends on this body-mind. So, as long as we live, there will be some identification with our body-mind machine and nothing is wrong with that. For example, our personal preferences will still come to the surface. But at the same time there is a 'knowing' – a knowing that does not come from the mind – a kind of 'seeing' that is shining through all this. That knowing is like a background that whispers, 'This body-mind machine has personal characteristics indeed, but it is not what I am'. And what happens, when we 'see' that? The natural preservation instincts will not disappear when our True Nature is seen. All the practical concerns to nurture and comfort the body, all the concepts we need to take care of ourselves and our fellow people will still be there. What changes is the judging voice inside. We can just be as we are and we are 'open' to what is, experiencing life as it presents itself. Then the concepts of a personal Enlightenment will lose their meaning completely.

When the spiritual seeker imagines he or she will finally get to the ego-less state, what will happen then? Who will be witnessing this enlightenment?[71] Does he or she expect a sense of enormous joy, an unbelievable sensation of divine Light? Many seekers secretly hope they will finally 'get' nirvana and be liberated for ever. All of that is of course impossible, although it is often presented as such in Eastern literature about Liberation. A person getting enlightenment is a contradiction in terms. As we said before, as long as there is a person there, as long as there is a concept about being liberated one day, as long as there is a clinging to some divine state, there is a person sitting in the middle of a whole lot of concepts. And what we are referring to is *conceptless*.

When we realize that all divisions on the Cosmic Screen are only illusory, we also know that an *individual* enlightenment is impossible because there is no separate being to become enlightened. As long as the seeker wishes to be there as a personal witness to his own awakening of this reality, he is not able to see this Consciousness. A seeker can never become a finder, simply because the finder must disappear first. As a result, we see that the (open) secret of rediscovering our True Nature is not hidden somewhere in the future or in some far exotic country. It is available right here, right now. All we have to do is leave behind our preconceptions and beliefs and forget ourselves while we embrace the present moment. Whatever we do or feel is not important, all that really matters is that we recognize the infinite in everyday life. All that is left is a divine embracing of what comes to the surface. It is as simple as breathing; we do not need a person claiming, 'Now I am breathing in and now I am breathing out'. Similarly, there is nothing we have to do in order to 'be what we are'. As pointed out before, there is no need to be special or spiritual in any way, there is no need to change our clothes, our name, our diet, our profession, our social position. When we think we have to change our lifestyle, that idea will only fortify the personality, stimulate its illusory idea of separation, and enhance our spiritual materialism.

When the seeking drops away, there is no longer the belief, 'I should be different'. The little devil inside who wants to make us belief that we are not worthy of Liberation, who says that our individual way of expressing our humanness is not good enough, is silent now. There is the clarity that everything and everyone is at it is. And that understanding is allowed now.

Transcendental events

Lift the stone and you will find me;
cleave the wood and I am there.

JESUS

Many people report mystical experiences that changed their lives profoundly. All their questions disappeared suddenly in a moment of openness. Some had It when they were with their master, others saw It when they were absorbed by the beauty of nature, others 'got it' when doing meditation. What is the value of all this? Is having such experiences an essential step to Liberation? Of course, yoga and formal meditation seem to alter awareness, but we should realize that it only changes our perception and not That which is perceiving. For example, when we focus within (e.g. when using spiritual techniques), we think that our awareness is 'higher' and since 'attaining a higher state of consciousness' is often presented as the goal of such spiritual disciplines, anything we do to serve this goal is considered spiritual and most important for the seeker. But this is a process that can go on and on. After each 'higher state of consciousness' there is another one waiting, still higher or profounder or more mysterious.

The problem with spiritual techniques and metaphysical knowledge is that people think these are positive signs of their spiritual growth. The ego likes that image very much, while in fact there is nobody to 'grow', there is nobody 'becoming more of what they already are'. All this knowledge and all these skills often serve to provide a very attractive diversion for the spiritual seeker on the path, and quite easily the seeker gets attached to his progress or starts to feel superior about his 'spiritual level'. Such elitist behaviour has nothing to do with the democratic spirituality we are referring to in this book.

When we become focused on a goal, like reaching higher states of consciousness, we think of consciousness as something we can control. We think of it as something which is personal, and which can be enhanced. Something which comes closer each time we have a mystical experience or a new spiritual insight. That is the dream of the wave who hopes to become the Pacific Ocean one day, without realizing that both the wave and the Ocean are water. Such belief systems keep us locked in a cycle of personal experiences: we feel happy when we have a peak experience, and we feel depressed when it is over. Although very attractive for the 'advanced' seeker, such a spiritual materialism has nothing to do with the Liberation we are referring to in this book.

So, what is the value of having transcendental experiences?

Are they tickets to paradise? Are they previews to Liberation? And what is their relationship to Naked Beingness? Nathan Gill[72] is very clear about this; he says that a special event comes and goes, that it may give direct insight into 'what is', but he also realizes that it is still an event, however blissful it was. A transcendental event can last a second or a minute, it may even seem to be there every day, but it is not a ticket for enlightenment. It is not an essential step for the spiritual seeker, although it can bring a lot of clarity in our quest. Many people state that such an event made clear what they never understood before. After the transcendental event(s), they seem to 'know' what it is all about, or at least see what others are pointing at. The whole issue becomes clear. In that way, these events *can* be important for the seeker. It can indeed take away a few – if not all – misconceptions and belief systems, but it is not obligatory in seeing our true nature. The hidden danger is that we want to own these events, we are disappointed when they are gone, or we feel frustrated that we haven't experienced any transcendental events in our own life. All these personal games are only tools for the ego to postpone its self-destruction.

Although many seekers report that the transcendental events in their life made them clear what 'It' is all about, there is also the danger that the ego wants to claim the central role again. This subtle way of avoiding the unmasking of the seeker is usually not recognised as such. Although mystical events can give new insights in the spiritual field, it can also be confusing. This appears to be true for some spiritual seekers/teachers. Several of them seem to have had important transcendental events *without* the understanding and clarity. That may become misleading when these people are now 'spreading the message' to help others in their quest. In some cases, these teachers present their own awakening as the standard, or copy the philosophy of their master. Their so-called mystic experiences are presented as most important, and their transcendental events are personalized in a very subtle way. Such teachings are very attractive for the spiritual seeker who wants to postpone the end of the spiritual search. Such teachings are still dualistic in their nature – although they are usually not recognized as such. And even this whole process (on the one hand desperately searching for It and on the other hand misleading ourselves) is also an expression of the Infinite. It is the way Consciousness plays the game of hide and seek. So in the end it doesn't matter, really.

NOBODY HOME?

> *Whoever one thinks one is,*
> *that disappears in the awakening.*[73]
> **ROBERT RABBIN**

The next experiment is quite an unusual one. Although the idea in itself is completely against all common sense, we really want to see – again – if there is a person inside our body. So we are invited to check out for ourselves if there is really somebody living inside our body. When we close our eyes for a few seconds, we can easily forget our name, our character. As we said before, we can understand that the concept of being a person with a specific name and characteristics is no more than a concept appearing in our awareness. In other words, it is an appearance. It is an idea which comes and goes, just like all the other ideas that come and go. It is clear that it is ridiculous to claim that what we really are is that idea – although everybody is doing so all the time. We are much more than just a concept, aren't we?

What we are is the awareness that allows all these ideas to

appear. That is what the spiritual teachers say. But common sense (vision X) still says we are a person. What is the truth, then? Can we really find a permanent 'person' somewhere inside ourselves? Can we find a little man or woman inside our brain? Is there a little person inside the sandcastle? Where does the ego live? In the skull? In the chest? In the belly? Let us take a look again, seriously. We can indeed notice that, on present evidence, it is not who we are but *that we are* which is significant. When we forget about vision X, we will find nobody is here. There is a Seeing process, yes, there are various things we cannotice (including images about ourselves), but that doesn't mean that these images represent what we are.

The fact that we can witness (parts of) the ego does not mean that our ego can claim the role of the Seer. And why can we say that? Well, the personality itself is part of the scenery, and as such not the Seer itself. The ego can never be the Seer. An object can never be the Subject. And as a result, the personality can never see the final Witness, just like a wave cannot see the Ocean. So, what happens during a seeing experiment or a transcendental event is simply the Subject seeing Itself! That is what we refer to in this book as 'Clear Seeing.' The personality is just a part of the scene that is being witnessed, but it is not the Witness. The ego always has the habit of claiming the central seat for himself or herself. In other words, the personality is just one of the objects, but not the Subject. To some, as we suggested before, seeing this emptiness at centre may feel uncomfortable. That is one of the reasons why this 'philosophy' will never become popular. Only those who want to go beyond the bottom line, are interested in this. Who wants to be Mr or Ms Nobody? Rediscovering who we really are can feel like disappearing, seeing the Centre of awareness may feel like annihilation of our personality, because it looks like a kind of death for the ego. As a person, we disappear, with nothing remaining at centre. But at the same time, we gain everything, because nothing is excluded. Then, we (as Consciousness, not as a person!) are a Space without any limits. Then there is real (impersonal) freedom.

THE SPECTRE IN THE LAKE

> *Each man is in his Spectre's power,*
> *until the arrival of that hour*
> *when his humanity awake*
> *and cast his own spectre into the lake.*
>
> **WILLIAM BLAKE**

We said that our body is a collection of perceptions, sensations and concepts put together by our memory, and that what we really are is the Final Witness of all these mental images. From that point of view, the body is also an image, a mental object. Likewise, the mind itself is also an object, but the Final Witness cannot be perceived because there would be another perceiver. Seeing that at centre we are not an appearance (not a body, not a mind) but a capacity for what happens is often described as a re-awakening to our original nature. This does not mean that we have to stop logical thinking, that we have to suppress our emotions or bodily sensations, or that we have to neglect the talents of our personality. This 'coming Home' does not make us change our lifestyle: we do not have to become different in any way. Waking up to this Clear Vision permits us to live life, just as before. We will not become special in any way, we will not become saints or perfect human beings. Nothing changes! So nobody will notice anything, we will not – in the view of others – become psychic or holy, but from our point of view [if we can still say that there is a trace of a personal point of view] *everything has changed.* For example, we see that the personality is just playing a game, and that this game is just a part of the big game of our First Person. We wake up from our daydream and see the role we are playing. This awareness goes beyond the idea of being a limited identity and offers the background in which this Beingness is directly and immediately available.

There is a famous Zen story that illustrates the recognition of the First Person vision wonderfully well.[74] It is a story of ten monks who discover their original face while looking at their reflection in the water of a pool. The ten monks had left their monastery and were travelling together from one Master to another, in search of enlightenment. While crossing a river, they were separated by the swift current. As none of them could swim, they were all afraid someone would drown. When finally they reached the other shore, the ten monks reassembled quickly. Immediately the leader of the group counted the other monks to make sure that all were safely across. Unfortunately, the monk was only able to count nine brothers because he overlooked himself. Then, a second monk also started to count, and made the same mistake: he also overlooked himself while counting and also ended up with counting nine friends instead of ten.

Each in turn counted the others, and each could only count nine brothers. So they all concluded one of them drowned in the river. As a result, they started bewailing their drowned brother. A passing traveller on his way to the nearest town asked what their trouble was. They explained one brother had drowned. But the traveller, having counted them, assured them that all ten were present [third person vision]. The monks did not believe him: each counted again and found only nine friends. When the traveller realized he was unable to persuade them they were still a group of ten monks and not nine, he gave up. He imagined they were out of their minds, left the ten monks and went on his way to town.

Then one monk left the group and went to a pool not far away from the river, in order to wash his face. As he leant over a rock above that little pool, he saw a human face. As he did not recognize this face as a reflection of his own face, he imagined that he had seen someone at the bottom of that pool. Since he believed he had discovered the drowned brother, he started back and, rushing to his fellow-monks, announced that he had found their poor drowned brother. So each in turn went over to that particular rock and, leaning over, looked into the depths of the pool. When all monks had seen their poor drowned brother (what they really saw was the reflection of their own face), they celebrated a funeral service in his memory. The same traveller, returning from town, asked them what they were doing. When he was told about the death of one monk, he tried to explain to them that each had celebrated his own death by looking at the reflection of his own face in the pool.

a. outsider's view
(third person vision)

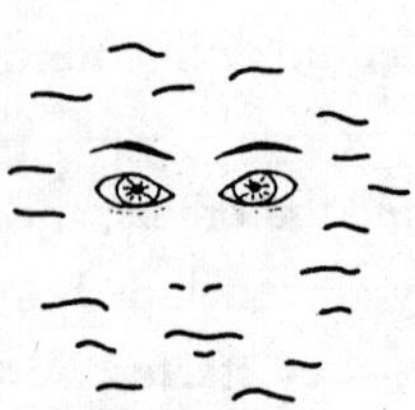

b. reflection
(second person vision)

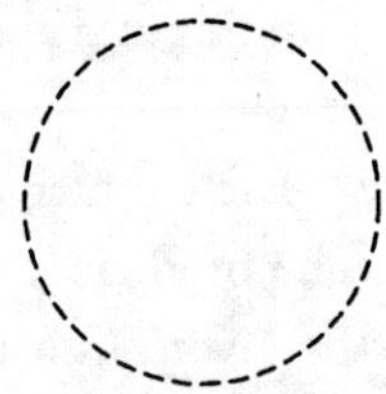

c. Original Face
(First Person vision)

He said to the monks that in fact all of them had seen their *own* death, the end of their own appearance (their second person) reflected in the pool. Now, the penny dropped. Each realized that he saw his appearance in the water and understood the difference between his face reflected in the pool (the second person) and the Original Face (the First Person). Although their second person seemed to have died, their First Person was alive and was now recognized as such. The story says that on seeing this each monk was instantly awakened.

11

BEING ONE

In the beginning
there was neither existence nor
non-existence,
all this world was unmanifest energy…
The One breathed, without breath
by Its own power.
Nothing else was there.

HYMN OF CREATION, THE RIG VEDA

IS ANYBODY THERE?

All the confusion was suddenly gone.
I knew Who or What I really am
without any shadow of a doubt
and it was obvious
that I already had been that
all my life.

NATHAN GILL

There is a story about a piano player that illustrates the importance of the discovery of the 'nobody-is-home' idea quite well. A man is a very famous piano player who lives in a beautiful country house facing a river. Every Sunday morning, at sunrise, he takes his little boat and makes a trip on the river, just to escape from the rush of everyday life for a few hours. He lets his boat float downstream and after a while, anchors it in the middle of the river. So he is sitting there in his little boat, in the very early morning. Nobody is around. He is staring into the water surface, enjoying the peace and silence of being in nature and doing nothing. While sitting there in peace, he couldn't stop wondering why people are always having trouble with each other. Hearing the sounds of the birds, looking at the colours of the sun reflected in the water, he considers how hard it is to believe why there is so much trouble in this world. He asks himself why we are always in confrontation with our neighbours and our friends.

Suddenly, his mind is disturbed by someone hitting his boat from behind. He starts, both surprised and angry at the same time and turns around, cursing. Then, in a timeless moment, he realizes that the boat he was hit by is empty! That he was yelling at... nobody. He understands that his boat had a collision with another boat coming from upstream. His anger disappears immediately and in a timeless flash, he is absorbed in a total stillness, which descends on everything. Oneness with all and everything is what happens and, at the same time, everything is enveloped in an all-encompassing love.

Afterwards, he realizes that this collision is a metaphor for the philosophical issues he had just been thinking about. All these other people we think we are having trouble with are just like empty boats. There is no captain in the other boats. Whatever they are doing, they can't help it. What an amazing discovery! Everybody on this planet is hypnotised by the common belief that we are all separate individuals, each living in a different body that walks around on the surface of the same planet. That is what we all believe, because we imagine that we 'have' a captain in our own boat. We all say, 'In my head, I have a captain who has free will and choice', and as a result we conclude, 'All the other bodies I see walking around, they look just like me, so they must have a captain, too'. And we are all hypnotised by this belief simply because it looks so real.

Everything is crystal clear now. His own boat too is floating around without a captain, just following the current that brings it where it is apparently going. In other words: he sees that 'his' body, which he always thought he was living in, is an empty box. It is like a radio playing piano music, without any pianist inside! Now he realizes, 'Nobody is living in this body, nobody is home! There is no captain in my boat, just as there are no captains in the other boats.' It only appears to be that way. And this recognition is also the end of his spiritual quest. The piano player really has to sit down for a moment, in order to take in the consequences of what has happened.

After sitting still like that for a while, he starts to get hungry.

His stomach calls him back into the 'real' world. The perfume of the stillness is still there, in the background, while 'he' is not there in the usual way. It is all amazing and quite common at the same time. He turns back home, rowing his boat upstream, to have breakfast. While he is drinking his coffee, he realizes that everything is *as it is*. No good, no bad, no past, no future, no now. How could it be so obvious, so simple and at the same time, nobody noticing it? The sound of the refrigerator, the smell of the coffee, the taste of the jam, everything is an expression of 'This'. He realizes that this Open Secret is beyond common understanding and although he would love to share this with all his friends, he realizes that he lacks the words to express 'This' to anyone. And even though his life changed that Sunday morning, never to be the same again, nobody ever noticed anything different about him. He plays the piano, just like before.

In this Garden of Eden we are all one

> ***Seeing that one is nothing, is wisdom;***
> ***seeing that one is everything, is love.***
>
> **NISARGADATTA MAHARAJ**

Mystics say that those who give their hopes and goals in the hands of the infinite awareness are left in a timeless presence because they let go their personal ambitions, they put in perspective their personal future, with nothing left to do. This may be referred to as Liberation, and the absolute freedom that it brings demands nothing from us. We can go on and live just as before. On the other hand, as long as we want to have anything *for ourselves*, especially spiritual freedom itself, we will not find true Liberation. This freedom is not for one individual, but is immediately there for all, even when those others do not recognize that Liberation as such.

Liberation is often described as a powerful blend of deep meditation, spiritual freedom, and the joy of finding unconditional love after a passionate inquiry. We all want the wonder that comes from finding ourselves drowned in a timeless and exhilarating free-fall of spiritual discovery, but such statements often suggest sensational experiences of bliss and, as a result, spiritual seekers are expecting similar blissful events. The problem is that many of us do not appreciate ordinary life any more. We are looking for ecstasy, for some higher state, for something special for ourselves. When we think about Liberation, it is important that we 'see' it in the common and the ordinary, and that we do not try to keep it as an award just for ourselves.

That Understanding is the end of all questions. Then, there is just Presence, then there is Clarity; no more others, no more past, no more future, no more doer, no more non-doer. Nobody is excluded now, even those who think or believe they are separate doers. All the concepts we believed in can still be there, but they have no more meaning. The seeking ends in the dissolution of the seeker. This goes with an unperceivable merging with Oneness, a complete falling away of dualism. It may go with a resonance with what is perceived (a book we read, a person we meet), but even that is not necessary. If we 'see' this, we may be freed from our identification, and our mask drops. However, the mask itself is not a problem, the problem is that we cling to that mask. So nothing is wrong with our personality, the point is that most of us identify exclusively with our personality. We have developed the habit of saying that this body-mind machine is all that we are. It is said that when that identification with the role we play disappears completely, we are free of all limitations. We melt away and expand to the endlessness of Consciousness. Then, it is said, we are in paradise. The latter does not mean that we are enlightened, that we become perfect human beings; we simply wake up from our daydream. At first, we think that we have discovered our Source, and we turn it into a personal experience; later we see that this is not really a personal experience, but rather the opposite: when the concept of being a person is *not* there, an impersonal awareness can come to the surface. It is the sandcastle discovering everything and everybody is made of sand. We may seem different in shape, but basically we are all the same.

We may also see that even when others are not conscious of it, they are also in contact with 'their' Source, as much as the most famous seer. Every castle is made of sand. Everybody lives from the same Source, everybody is at Home anyway, and this is independent of behaviour or descent, independent of realizing it or not, willing it or not. We could conclude, 'The Light that lets 'my film' shine is the same Light – or originates from the same Source – as the light that lets your film shine'. This insight makes the seer a bit more modest: this consciousness is not only free for everyone, and available at any time, but it is for everyone the one and same Light. In this Garden of Eden there are no more separate beings, we are all one. We all share this consciousness: this Home is our common good. In this Space, there are no more separate persons! This insight can become the basis for unattached friendship, for true compassion, for unconditional love, because the difference between me and the other, the distance between you and me, is completely dissolved. In fact, we are all the same on several levels. On the atomic level, we are all the same because we are all made of molecules which are made of atoms. And these atoms are in fact empty space filled with neutrons and electrons. On the metaphysical level, we are also the same because we all share this Consciousness. We all 'look through' this same Light, and we do not need any book to see this. Just look in the eyes of your fellow people, and you will 'see' your Self, reflected in their eyes. The Bhagavad Gita says:

> He who sees the supreme Lord
> dwelling alike in all beings,
> and never perishing when they perish,
> he sees indeed.

ONE CONSCIOUSNESS

> ***Recognize the magical show of appearances***
> ***as reflections of your own thoughts.***
> ***Know your own mind as empty by nature –***
> ***no need to seek elsewhere for the bliss of reality!*** [75]
>
> **TANTRIC SONG**

Earlier in this book, when asking questions like, 'Is there a person living in this body?' we finally came to a blank Space. There is not much to say any more. We also realize that all the words in this book will never succeed in describing this Space. When our true nature is seen, we are absorbed in a borderless room where nothing is left. When we (who?) stay there, we can just wonder what it is like to be this Clear Emptiness.[76] As we suggested before, many seekers still expect that once they have finally found Liberation, they will always feel calm and peaceful.

However, it is not a rule that once we have recognized our awareness, that all problems will go away. Liberation does not guarantee freedom from pain and suffering. Why should we believe that? Not one so-called awakened being is without problems, not one spiritual teacher is more awake than you and I. How could they, if there is only one Consciousness? How could anyone ever claim the best part of consciousness for himself and leave the rest for the others? Consciousness cannot be divided into pieces like a pizza; it is One and all-encompassing. So we do not have to imitate the spiritual heroes, we can be ourselves just the way we are right now. Trying to change our way of life is another barrier, indeed. True recognition of being already awake can occur in our ordinary living: there is no need to look any deeper than plain everyday life. Tony Parsons said:[77] 'This is about an intimacy, a love affair, total poverty, total humility. Something which is utterly beyond detachment.'

If we are looking for the infinite, there can only be one of it and not two or more. In that case, the way the infinite consciousness is expressing itself through each of us, is already It. This means that the way Consciousness expresses itself during a 'normal' activity (eating, writing, working in the garden, driving) is as valid as the way consciousness expresses itself in some kind of blissful state. It may express itself in peace or fear, in joy or depression, and so on. It is all equally consciousness. Believing the inner voice who says we should be different doesn't matter any more. As Nathan Gill[78] says, 'Being identified with the ego or not, who cares?'

If all these processes of the mind are checkmated, what is left of us? When we have lost our tools (believing, contemplating, meditating, logical thought), what is there left to do? If we are in an ego-less state or experiencing bliss, that is It.

If we are holding this book in our hands, then the sensation of feeling the pressure in our hands is It. If we are taking an aspirin to get rid of our headache, that is It. If we are dying from a terrible disease, that is It. All are equally expressions of the infinite. Liberation is available right now and we can do nothing about it to get it, and we are not able to chase it away.

It is completely useless to try and rid ourselves of anything. Why should we try and be in a divine state? Why should we judge our personality, or even try to be without an ego? The naked Consciousness is not interested in evaluating what arises in It, just as the TV screen is not judging the actors on the screen for what they say or do. Every path which suggests that there is something wrong with the world is a subtle way of postponing the bare fact that everything is as-it-is. Every teacher who suggests that there is something wrong with what we think or feel or do is only fortifying our belief that we should be different from what we are. We pray hoping to be blessed, we meditate hoping to become enlightened, but it is all a game within a game, and as such completely ridiculous. Our minds create an image of a better future, and like hamsters running in our caged exercise wheel, we are only pretending to go from one place to another, while in fact we are not going anywhere.[79]

Once we have understood these mechanisms, there is absolutely no need anymore to go into a temple and meditate because exactly where we are right now, is meditation. Whatever we feel or do is the expression of the infinite. We are all exactly as we are supposed to be. And as soon as it is seen that everything is as it is, and that there is nothing wrong with *what is*, that nothing or nobody needs to be ameliorated, all our past efforts to become more spiritual are now seen for what they are: completely useless.[80] All these spiritual techniques are now as relevant as the toys we used to play with as a young child: most important and very interesting at that time, but now they have no more meaning at all.

BEING HOME

Nothing happened to me
under the bodhi tree.
Absolutely nothing.

GAUTAMA BUDDHA

If coming Home is about finding our True Nature in the simplicity of *what is* as it is, we may wonder if, in the end, we have arrived exactly where we came from. Consciousness will appear to seduce us and to amaze us by using our minds to create a virtual world. But in the end Consciousness is not separate from what we perceive, it is not separate from us, it *is* us. When we fully embrace It as our true nature, we joyously welcome it with a sense of deep gratitude and profound wonderment. It is a miraculous gift that Consciousness is giving to Itself. It is Consciousness coming Home to Itself. When that is seen, there is a clarity about what we are, and about what life is all about. Now we know that we do not have to change our lifestyle in order to see This. What can water do to become wet? What may Consciousness try to do in order to become conscious? Let us see it this way: if the Self is what we really are, how could there ever be a time when we were apart from the Self? The magic is already here. As a result, trying to make our life more spiritual is just a matter of avoiding clarity, indeed. It is already happening, consciousness is already creating our world right now. And we are that! We do not have to wait for a transcendental event to occur to recognize that we are already an expression of the infinite. We do not have to imitate a spiritual hero. We can recognize our true nature in what is happening right here. This unconditional love is fully available right now. It is there while we are reading this chapter. Yes, exactly now while our mind is perceiving these words. All the perceptions that come into our awareness right now: that is It. Seeing what appears in our mind as it is, without any comments, that is what we call 'being Home'.

As long as we think we are a seeker, the *invitation* to come Home is always there, in whatever we perceive. And the joke is that we don't need to come Home because we are already Home anyway. Then, there is nowhere to go. Then, everything is a *celebration* of the Infinite. No more words are necessary now. The way the Infinite expresses Itself does not need any embellishment: the simplicity of 'what is' is more than sufficient.

But all these descriptions weigh heavy on the all-encompassing transparency of the actual moment. Theories and words are unnecessary because the Clarity is available in the most ordinary aspects of life. Words can only hide the Transparency that is there anyway. First Person vision shows that there is no need to find our way back to the Source, because we already are that Source we are longing for. In other words: Home is ever-present right here. What happens then, when Home comes Home? Externally, nothing changes, but internally, our vision of certain things has changed: we have seen the infinite in the simplest aspects of life. It even doesn't matter if we have transcendental events or not, it doesn't matter if we feel separate or free, it is all the infinite expression anyway. And as a result, we are back where we started. In Zen, the following story is told: Before you start with Zen, you see rivers and mountains as rivers and mountains. When you are occupied for a while with

Zen, rivers are no longer rivers and mountains are no longer mountains. And finally, the rivers and mountains are rivers and mountains again.

So we do not have to go anywhere, because the Infinite is always available, nothing needs to be added, nobody needs to be changed in order to be ready for It. It may have been confusing or liberating to see through a number of illusions. But in essence, we have returned to the place where we started, and maybe this journey is also an illusion. Ramana Maharshi says it all:

> There is no greater mystery than this, that we keep seeking reality though in fact are reality. We think that there is something hiding reality and that this must be destroyed before reality is gained. How ridiculous! A day will dawn when you will laugh at all your past efforts. That which will be the day you laugh is also here and now.

Bibliography

Adams R: *When you see Emptiness Inside Yourself*, Self Enquiry, vol. 8, N° 1, April 2000, pp.16–22

Ardagh N (Arjuna): *How About Now?* Grass Valley, California: Self X Press, 1999

Balsekar R: *Who cares?!*, Redondo Beach (CA), Advaita Press, 1999

Blackburn S: *Think – A Compelling Introduction to Philosophy*, Oxford, New York: Oxford University Press, 1999

Chopra D: *The Way of the Wizard*, New York: Harmony Books, 1995

Combs A: *The Radiance Of Being*, St. Paul, Minnesota: Paragon House, 1996

Deida D: *Finding God through Sex*, Austin: Plexus, 2000

Gill N: *Clarity*, Maidstone: G.O.B. Publications, 2000

Gill N: 'I am On It', Self Enquiry, vol. 8, N° 1, April 2000, pp.38–9

Harding DE: *Face To No-Face*, Carlsbad (California): Innerdirections Publishing, 2000

Harding DE: *Look For Yourself*; London: Head Exchange Press, 1996

Harrison S: *Getting To Where You Are*, New York: Tarcher/Putnam, 1999

Hillig C: Enlight*enment For Beginners*, Ojai (California): Black Dot Publications, 1999

Hillig C: *The Way It Is*, Ojai (California): Black Dot Publications, 2001

Kersschot J: *Coming Home*, Aartselaar (Belgium): Inspiration, 2000

Klein J: *Transmission of the Flame*, Third Millennium Publications, St Peter Port (Guernsey, C.I.), 1990

Lang R: *An Illustrated Guide*, London: Head Exchange Press, 1994

Liquorman W: *Acceptance of What Is*, Redondo Beach (CA): Advaita Press, 2000

Lucille F: *Eternity Now*, Middletown: Truespeech Productions, 1996

Lumiere LM, Lumiere-Wins J: *The Awakening West*, Oakland, Clear Visions Publications, 2000

Menon, Krishna: *Atma-Nirvriti*, Trivandrum, S. India: Vedanta Publishers, 1952

Nitschke G: *The Silent Orgasm*, Köln: Taschen, 1995

Parsons T: *The Open Secret*, Sancreed, Penzance: The Connections, 1995/1998

Parsons T: *As It is, Dialogues on The Open Secret*, UK: Open Secret Publishing, 2000

Parsons T: *As It is*, Carlsbad (CA): Innerdirections Publishing, 2000

Ramana Maharshi: *The Collected Works of Ramana Maharshi*, edited by Arthur Osborne, York Beach: Samuel Weiser, 1997

Ramana Maharshi: *The Spiritual Teaching of Ramana Maharshi*, Boston & London: Shambala, 1988

Ramana Maharshi: *Conscious Immortality*, Conversations with Ramana Maharshi, published by V.S. Ramanam, Tiruvannamalai 1998

Ram Tzu: *No Way*, Redondo Beach (CA): Advaita Press, 1999

Roberts B: *The Experience of No-Self*: A Contemplative Journey (revised edn), State University of New York Press, Albany, 1993

Rumi: Birdsong: *Fifty-Three Short Poems*, Athens: Maypop, 1993

Rumi: *The Love Poems of Rumi*, edited by D. Chopra, Harmony Books, New York, 1998

Schoegl I: *The Zen Teaching of Rinzai*, Berkeley: Shambhala, 1976

Tolle E, *The Power of Now*, Novato (CA): New World Library, 1999

Toshio Sudeo P: *Zen Sex – The Way of Making Love*, New York: HarperCollins, 2000

Watts A: *Buddhism, The Religion of No-Religion*, Boston: Tuttle Publishing, 1999

Wei Wu Wei: *The Tenth Man*, Hong Kong University Press, 1966

Wilber K: *One Taste*, Boston: Shambhala Publications 1998

Zetty M: *Reflections on Awakening*, AIA E-zine no. 4: May 1999

Text Credits

Grateful acknowledgement is made to the publishers and authors who kindly gave permission to reprint material from the following books and articles:

Ardagh N (Arjuna): *How About Now?* Self X Press, 1999

Blazwick I and Wilson S, *The Tate Modern Handbook*, Tate Publishing, London, 2000

Deida D: *Finding God through Sex*, Plexus, 2000

Gill N: *Clarity*; G.O.B. Publications, 2000

Harding DE: *Face To No-Face*, Carlsbad (California): Innerdirections Publishing, 2000

Harding DE : *Look For Yourself*; London: Head Exchange Press, 1996

Harding DE: *The Little Book of Life and Death*, Arkana, 1988

Hillig C: *Enlightenment For Beginners*, Black Dot Publications, 1999

Hillig C: *The Way It Is*, Black Dot Publications, 2001

Kersschot J: *Coming Home*, Inspiration, 2000: See also www.kersschot.com

Liquorman W: *Acceptance of What Is*, Advaita Press, 2000

Lumiere LM, Lumiere-Wins J: *The Awakening West*, Clear Visions Publications, 2000

Mark McCloskey: www.puresilence.org

Parsons T: *The Open Secret*, 1995

Parsons T: *As It Is, Dialogues on The Open Secret*, The Open Secret Publishing, 2000

Parsons T: As It Is, Innerdirections Publishing, 2000

Shaw M: *Passionate Enlightenment: Women in Tantric Buddhism*, Princeton University Press, 1994

Vervoordt A, *The Story of a Style*, Assouline Publishing, 2001

Watts *A: Buddhism, The Religion of No-Religion;* Boston: Tuttle Publishing, 1999

Zetty M: www.awakening.net

Notes

1 This Awareness should be differentiated from attention. Our attention can wander from one sense to another, or travel up and down the inside of our body; now focusing on our tongue and next on some muscular tension in our neck. Awareness is That which is aware of attention shifting from here to there, from this to that. Our attention seems to 'move' all the time, but Awareness remains still and unmovable. Wherever we are, whatever appears in our attention, there It is, open to what is.

2 Most of these experiments are borrowed from the English philosopher Douglas Harding.

3 *The Open Secret*, Penzance: The Connections, 1995/1998, p. 2

4 See also: www.theopensecret.com

5 See also: Steven Harrison: *Getting To Where You Are*, New York: Tarcher/Putnam, 1999, pp. 46-7

6 This reminds me of what Mark McCloskey said: 'I have a challenge for you. For this moment, give up your belief in anything. Have courage and let go all that you have been taught. For one moment let go of your religion with its creeds and gods and sins and saviours. Let go of every thought. Even this one. As hard as it is or appears to be, let go of your religious belief completely. What is a religious belief? It is the thoughts of some other human being written down or followed or theologised by others. Do you want to follow the thoughts of others or do you want to be free? You cannot do both. Do you want to find that to which all true teachers are pointing or do you want to follow the crowds with their traditions, ideologies and demands or the hierarchies with their power, control and wealth? Stop it all right now and see what is left, see what is still in you, independent of any belief and yet encompassing all beliefs.' See also: www.puresilence.org

7 *Clarity*, GOB Publications 2000, p. 27

8 See also Ramesh Balsekar, *Who Cares?!*, Advaita Press, 1999, p. 79, and p. 81

[9] DE Harding : *Look For Yourself*, London: Head Exchange Press, 1996

[10] LM Lumiere & Lumiere-Wins J: *The Awakening West*, Clear Visions Publications, 2000, p. 287

[11] See also *Enlightenment For Beginners*, Black Dot Publications 1999 (www.blackdotpubs.com)

[12] See also www.theopensecret.com

[13] See also 'The Joy of Sharing' Interview with Mira Pagal in: *Coming Home*, Inspiration, 2001, pp. 358–68

[14] According to vision X, language is just a tool for communication, but according to vision Y thoughts (and thus language) are a subtle way of the mind to bring into existence a so-called 'real world'. The latter means that the 'reality' we talk about is actually *produced* by thoughts. And we get a 'common world' by agreeing on the way we describe it. In other words, by labelling the world around us, we get a standardized concept of the world using language. At a certain point, it is hard to find out if there are first the thoughts and then the objects, or first the objects and then the thoughts. All we can presume is that both seem to appear at the same time.

[15] Tony Parsons in Hampstead, London, August 2001, audiotape © Tony Parsons, www.theopensecret.com

[16] See also: *The Spiritual In Art: Abstract Painting 1890–1985*, Los Angeles County Museum of Art; Abbeville Press Publishers New York, 1986: p. 377

[17] Wayne Liquorman: *Acceptance Of What Is*, Advaita Press, California, 2000, p. 138

[18] See also: www.headless.org

[19] Unfortunately, as Galileo discovered when his inquisitors refused to look through his telescope, we cannot share 'This' with those readers who are not really interested.

[20] See also: DE Harding, *Face To No-Face, Rediscovering Our Original Nature*, ed. David Lang, Innerdirections, Carlsbad (CA), 2000, p.189 (www.innerdirections.org)

[21] See also www.headless.org/experiments.htm

22 See also Harding, *Face To No-Face, Rediscovering Our Original Nature*

23 In *Surrealism and Painting*, 1928

24 See also Jan Kersschot, *Coming Home*, p. 24 (www.inspiration.yucom.be/cominghome.htm)

25 Tony Parsons In Hampstead, London August 2001

26 see also: www.puresilence.org

27 See also Chuck Hillig, *The Way "It" Is*, Black Dot Publications, 2001

28 Ibid., p. 91

29 Tony Parsons in Hampstead, London August 2001

30 Lumiere, *The Awakening West*, p. 185

31 See also: http://awakening.net/Ezine.html

32 *The Open Secret:* the Connections 1999, p. 47

33 Everything which appears on the Screen will disappear again. What is born will die. There is something amazing and wonderful about this eternal play of creation and destruction and, at the same time, it looks tragic. That is where the Hindu conception of Kali, the Black Goddess, is so relevant. One hand creates the universe and the other hand destroys it. This concept of eternal creation and destruction is not only found in the Hindu tradition, it can also be recognized in contemporary art. It is just a matter of recognizing it. The same idea – the continuous creation and destruction of the universe – is for example expressed in some paintings by Fontana. Lucio Fontana (1899–1968) made many monochrome paintings with one or more cuts, representing Fontana's transgressive assault on rationality and taste (in *Tate Modern The Handbook*, eds Iwona Blazwick and Simon Wilson, Tate Publishing, London, 2000, p. 155). And although we don't know if Fontana ever created his works of art with this idea in mind, these works can have the following symbolic meaning: the monochrome canvas can be seen as a symbol for the creation, in Hinduism presented by Brahman and the slicing gestures can be seen as a symbol for the destruction, in Hinduism presented by Shiva.

34 See also Nathan Gill, *Clarity*

35 in *The Open Secret*, pp. 46–47

36 Kasimir Malevich (1878–1935) stood for the principle of Non-Objectivity, which means not painting pictures of the objects of the world but abstractions that symbolize dynamic energy, universal space and cosmic order. One of his most famous paintings, *Black Square* (1913) was first exhibited in 1915 and is considered as the first icon of Suprematism. 'I have transformed myself in the zero of forms and gone beyond zero', he wrote in the manifesto which he handed out to visitors of that exhibition in 1915. Since then, representing 'nothingness' has been a constant presence in Modern art. Although unpopular among the general public, we have seen a steady stream of radical blanks and monochrome voids in the twentieth century. See also: Matthew Collings, *This Is Modern Art*, London: Seven Dials, 2000, pp. 144 & 159.

37 Barnett Newman (b. USA 1905–70), one of the principal artists to be associated with Abstract Expressionism, said (in *Tate Modern The Handbook*, p. 56): 'For me space is where I can feel four horizons, not just the horizon in front of me and in back of me because then the experience of space exists only as volume… Anyone standing in front of my paintings must feel the vertical domelike vaults encompass him to awaken an awareness of his being alive in the sensation of complete space.'

38 Mark Rothko (b. 1903–70) was said to be a deeply spiritual man. He is sometimes referred to as 'the tragic artist of nothingness'. His paintings were soft and formless and emphasized colour (see also Matthew Collings, *This Is Modern Art*, pp. 166–9). In order to be able to be 'absorbed' by both the 'fullness' and the 'emptiness' in their paintings, both Rothko and Newman invite the spectator to stand close to their works of art. See also: J Golding, *Paths to the Absolute*, London: Thames and Hudson, 2000 (National Gallery of Art, Washington): p. 222.

39 The French artist Yves Klein (1928–62) is especially interesting here for his monochrome blue paintings. The blue he used was said to be symbolic of 'the Void', which was arrived at by passing through a zero zone. Klein wrote, 'Having rejected nothingness, I

discovered the Void.' See Collings, *This Is Modern Art*, p. 170.

40 Reinhardt made his first monochromes in the 1950s, initially painted in blue or red. In the late fifties, he executed black monochromes, where ghostly squares were just visible through the pigment (see Collings, *This Is Modern Art*, pp. 155–6).

41 The invitation to transcend the senses and to offer a glimpse of the Infinite can also be recognized in some works of art by Anish Kapoor (b. Bombay, 1954). See, e.g., his work *At the Edge of the World* (1998), which invites the spectator to melt away in a completely new sense of space. See also: Axel Vervoordt, *The Story of a Style*, New York: Assouline Publishing, 2001, pp. 162–3. Kapoor uses a deep red pigment to cover an eight metre wide dome, which leaves the visitor with a dazzling sense of space. Similar to what spectators describe when standing in front of a painting of Rothko or Newman, there can be both a sense of void and of fullness. The use of dense red pigmentation dematerialises the sculptural form so that presence and absence are simultaneously suggested. Such a union of opposites exemplifies the sense of 'empty wholeness' which Kapoor seems to invoke throughout his work (see also *The Tate Modern Handbook*, p. 183). Some authors even refer to his sculptures as contemporary works of Tantric art (see also Edward Lucie-Smith in: *Visual Arts in the Twentieth Century*).

42 See also *The Spiritual In Art: Abstract Painting 1890–1985*, p. 133 (fig. 2)

43 Kahlil Gibran in *The Prophet*

44 See also: 'The Invitation is Always There' First interview with Tony Parsons in *Coming Home*, pp. 331–41

45 *The Open Secret*, pp. 4–5

46 Lumiere, The *Awakening West*, p. 283

47 See also Chuck Hillig, *Enlightenment For Beginners*

48 in *The Open Secret*, p. ii

49 see also photo on front cover of *Coming Home*

50 in *Clarity*, p. 19

51 See also 'You are Space for my face', an interview with Douglas Harding in *Coming Home*, pp. 342–8

52 in the foreword to *Finding God through Sex* by David Deida, Plexus, 2000

53 It is our Natural State, something that we simply recognize for what it is: the empty space for all our experiences. As such, it is not a state.

54 see also *Finding God through Sex*. According to Deida, our male energy wants to get lost in physical ecstasy (while disappearing for the partner), and our female energy wants to be loved by the partner as the all-encompassing Love-energy (while opening our heart completely). But in the end, all this doesn't matter if we see that a real Tantric encounter is not about claiming personal achievements.

55 See also http://awakening.net/Ezine.html

56 We usually believe that 'we' create thoughts, that there is a thinker inside who chooses our thoughts. But maybe it is the other way around: the so-called thinker is only a concept, an idea. In other words: thoughts create the thinker. And if we 'feel' as if we are really choosing, that is only what our inner voice suggests. And the latter is again a mental image. In other words, there is only an *apparent* choice.

57 As soon as we realize that the ego – who feels helpless and hopeless – is in itself an illusion, nothing matters any more. Where should we go, if everything is an expression of Consciousness?

58 Tony Parsons in Hampstead, August 2001

59 See also *Coming Home*, pp. 231–43

60 See *Face To No-Face, Rediscovering Our Original Nature*, pp. 87–8

61 See *Paths To The Absolute*

62 See *The Spiritual In Art: Abstract Painting 1890 –1985*, p. 233

63 See also www.theopensecret.com

64 The danger is that after the peak experience the seeker starts to look for the experience of bliss again. He or she misses this taste of inner peace of the first impact. As a result, the mind divides life into a divine part on the one hand and the usual day-to-day life on the other. But the seeker does not understand that even

without the mind's interpretation, the world as it appears in day-to-day life *is* undivided, and as such already whole (See also *Getting To Where You Are*, p. 207). In other words: there is no need at all to be a 'seer' who notices this Oneness permanently. There is no need at all to be in a higher state all the time. And why is that? Well, there are three reasons for that. First, It is not personal. Second, It is beyond our concepts of time, and third, It cannot be experienced.

65 In a telephone conversation with the author, November 2001.

66 See also *Getting To Where You Are*, p. 91

67 See www.nathangill.com

68 Tony Parsons in Hampstead, August 2001

69 See also (in Dutch): Justus Kramer Schippers, *Leven Vanuit Neutraliteit*, Panta Rhei (Holland), 1997

70 in *The Open Secret*, p. 25

71 See *The Way "It" Is*

72 See 'Making It Clear', interview with Nathan Gill in *Coming Home*, pp. 369–83

73 Lumiere, *The Awakening West*, p. 28

74 Wei Wu Wei, *The Tenth Man*, Hong Kong, Hong Kong University Press, 1966

75 Miranda Shaw, *Passionate Enlightenment: Women in Tantric Buddhism*, Princeton, Princeton University Press, 1994, p. 93

76 When we sit and watch ourselves carefully, the only thing we can do is this: we discover that there is nothing we can do. And as Tony Parsons says, *that is a discovery*! This Liberation is so simple, that it comes without any effort or belief.

77 Tony Parsons in Hampstead, August 2001

78 See 'Making It Clear' in *Coming Home*, pp. 369–83

79 See *Coming Home*, pp. 177–84

80 See also *Getting To Where You Are*, p. 97